Endorsements for
Amity in the Middle East

"I have been consistently encouraged by the work of Conflict Prevention through sport by Geoffrey Whitfield and his colleagues. Their successful work in Israel with Arab and Jewish young people has been the result of both vision and sustained hard work. The story will encourage and activate everyone interested and involved in peace work." *Desmond M. Tutu, Archbishop Emeritus*

"There's much talk about conflict resolution; less about conflict prevention, and even then, it tends to be in the rarefied realms of conferences and consultations. Other than the fact it is a good read, there are three reasons why this book is important. It deals with conflict resolution at ground level; it involves the generations whose futures are in the melting-pot, and it's about sport – which is not just fun, but is where people learn about justice, fair play, obeying the rules and team work." *Colin M. Morris, Head of Broadcasting, BBC Northern Ireland*

"Geoffrey Whitfield is a British minister of religion and I am an American Arab writer. We have nothing in common other than a passion to 'ignite' peace in the Middle East. My approach is to write books that tell the truth, clearly, honestly without fear or compromise. By the time I finished reading *Amity in the Middle East* I realized that no matter how good my writing might be, if I stopped there I was leaving half of my job undone. *Amity* is a factual account of how an idealized vision was transformed into a reality. Ultimately, it is a 'manual' that serves as a guide to others with similar ambitions.

Whitfield's dream was to create a self-perpetuating situation in which Arab and Jewish youngsters would learn to understand and trust each other by playing football – 'soccer'. Intense competition pitting nation-against-nation often degenerates into a war without guns. Whitfield, simply but ingeniously, avoided that pitfall by not only making each team part Arab, part Jewish, but also part male, part female. The shared vision – democratic, passionate, and rife with difficulties and pitfalls – is an expression of religion as passionate action. Imagine, if you can, the glorious incongruity of Arab and Jewish boys and girls playing soccer in Bethlehem or Nazareth, or in the shadow of the Sermon on the Mount. Downright inspiring." *Ron David, author of* Arabs & Israel for Beginners

"This is a record of a wonderful experiment – peace made manifest through the monumental efforts, shared vision and 'practical faith' of a Working Group keenly committed to serving generations to come. The book reads more like a suspense novel as Geoffrey documents the birth and growth of WSPP, the impossible made possible by the involvement of people who 'have a scale of mind and heart beyond the ordinary'. Football (soccer) is a powerful metaphor for learning to trust, having confidence in each other, and working together toward a common goal . . . behaviors which continue to be all too elusive on a global scale. In deference to Forrest Gump, 'Peace is as peace does'. Geoffrey, David and their colleagues have <u>done</u> it!" *J. Clayton Schroeder, bookseller and freelance writer, Portsmouth, NH, USA*

"This is a heartwarming story of hope which is in the end not about sport, but about people." *Mark Woods, Editor, Baptist Times*

Amity in the
Middle East

Amity in the Middle East

How the World Sports Peace Project and the
Passion for Football brought together Arab and
Jewish Youngsters

GEOFFREY WHITFIELD

THE ***A**lpha* PRESS

BRIGHTON • PORTLAND

2 4 6 8 10 9 7 5 3 1

First published 2006 in Great Britain by
THE ALPHA PRESS
PO Box 139, Eastbourne BN24 9BPP

and in the United States of America by
THE ALPHA PRESS
920 NE 58th Ave   Suite 300
Portland, Oregon 97213–3786

British Library Cataloguing in Publication Data

A CIP catalogue record for this book is available from the British Library.

Library of Congress Cataloging-in-Publication Data
Whitfield, Geoffrey.
Amity in the middle east: how the World Sports Peace
Project and the passion for football brought together
Arab and Jewish youngsters / by Geoffrey Whitfield.
p. cm.
Includes bibliographical references and index.
ISBN 1-898595-48-8 (p/b : alk. paper)
1. Sports—Political aspects. 2. Soccer—Political aspects.
3. World Sports Peace Project. I. Title.

GV706.35.W45 2006
306.4'83—dc22

2006014426

Typeset and designed by G&G Editorial, Brighton & Eastbourne
Printed by The Alden Press, Oxford
This book is printed on acid-free paper.

Contents

Foreword
by David Bedford

I little realised in 2000 that a phone call from my old college chaplain of more than 30 years ago, Geoff Whitfield, would give me so much work to do for the next four years. Nor that it would lead me into an enterprise which could affect hundreds of Jewish and Arab youngsters in Israel at a time when there was bloodshed and violence. He rang me up out of the blue one day and I invited him to have lunch. He outlined a project for which he wanted my views and thoughts. He told me he had been working in Israel with kids for a number of years and wanted to start a project for Arabs and Jews in which they could play football in combined teams. If they were to win they would have to leave aside the old animosities, learn to trust each other and play together as a team. That could provide an alternative to the conflict and, if successful, could go through the country and to anywhere in the world. The consequences could be massive and bring about changes in relationships that could have a lasting effect in the country. Imagine the difference if Ariel Sharon and Yasser Arafat had been able to sit down, look at each other and say: "Didn't we play football together?" It seemed so simple: I said to him, "This could take off". Only then did I mention to him that some of my contacts through the Flora London Marathon might be able to help.

With another friend, Alan Pook from Brighton, we had to raise a team of volunteer coaches, obtain funds to cover the costs and run the project for a week every summer. We knew that if it was successful we would have to find a big organisation to take it over. The trouble was that we had never done anything like it before, and nor had anyone else. We enlisted a working group and worked our socks off. Even though no one was paid, the cost of equipment, flights and other expenditure was immense and had to be raised.

This book tells something of the story and how it has become so successful. Our first project in 2001 had one hundred kids, but almost a thousand took part in 2005. Volunteers from six universities have taken part and some twenty Jewish and Arab towns in Israel are involved. We could not have done it without them, plus a host of invisible helpers and others well known, like the University of Brighton, the British Embassy, the British Council, the Israel Sports Authority and Arsenal Football Club. After three successful summers, we entrusted it to the University of Brighton and the British Council.

I have done many memorable things in my life, but this has been one of the most important things I have ever had the pleasure of being a part of. Just beware of chaplains! They never leave you alone for long!

DAVID BEDFORD D.Sc., Director, Flora London Marathon

Prologue

Who is this book intended for? For those wanting to read an impossible dream of an antidote to terrorism and violence that happened; about Arab and Jewish youngsters playing football together and having a whale of a time, year on year, instead of what happens elsewhere; for those wanting to read about sport, especially football, and how it can bring people together instead of separating them; for those interested in conflict prevention and peace-making; for those wanting to be involved, or even to run such a project. So this book is for youngsters, parents, grandparents, sportspeople, students, teachers, peacemakers, radicals, politicians, church people, non-church people, business people, philanthropists, project workers, community and youth workers, theologians, leaders of all persuasions and faiths – and Israelis and Palestinians.

This is a true story of one man's perception of working in Israel with Arab and Jewish young people from separate communities in the region of Galilee. After he had worked voluntarily in Israel and the West Bank from 1993, things changed dramatically in 2000. That was the time when there were stories of violence and terrorism between Jews and Arabs, and which led to a meeting between Geoffrey Whitfield and his friend, David Bedford of the Flora London Marathon. Over three years, they created a successful Football/Conflict Prevention Project which took place on an annual basis, close to Nazareth.

The project, with roots planted in the invisible soil of theological and political insight, eventually brought together hundreds of youngsters and adults from a number of towns in Israel, staff and students from four English universities, Premier League clubs, especially Arsenal Football Club, the British Embassy and the British Council in Israel, the Israel Sports Authority, runners in the Flora London Marathon and a host of largely invisible donors. It became a pointer to more creative ways for community relations in divided societies.

It was ready to go to Bethlehem in the West Bank in the summer of 2002 until prevented by the Israeli invasion in March which followed the Al Aqsa Intifada of September 2001, but one day it will happen. It could go anywhere in the world, and anyone with vision and commitment could do it. After three successful, ever-growing projects between 2001 and 2003, its future development in 2004 and thereafter, was formally entrusted to the British Council in Israel and the University of Brighton in the UK, and renamed F4P.

Those who took part will tell their children and grandchildren of the time when Jews and Arab Christians and Arab Moslems played in mixed teams against mixed teams. Their team could win when they learned to work together and above all, create trust and confidence in each other. With such a model, the future of the peoples could have hope, and not despair.

Hopefully this book will not simply tell its own amazing story but provide others with a model to be used as a manual as they undertake pioneering projects themselves. Moreover, hopefully, it will enthuse organisations and individuals in giving proactive support to creative experiments and "impossible dreams".

Preface

It was Carrie Elsam of Ringmer, East Sussex, who suggested over a lunch during Christmas 2000 that Geoffrey should write a manual, after he had said how he regretted that no manual existed to help him with the work that he was contemplating in Israel and Palestine. She said: "You should write it!" It was her prompting that was responsible for this attempt to tell the story, rather than a manual, showing the golden thread of what some might call a remarkable string of 'coincidences'. Or was it not really much more to do with the unseen hand of God? It had started from a simple, uncomplicated beginning in a Hampshire village in 1993, to eventual international complexity and significance in 2000 and thereafter.

The story is written in the third person, despite the well-intended criticism of many, probably to eliminate the embarrassment of the writer. The project came to be seen as a non-governmental organisation, entitled the World Sports Peace Project, and the initials, WSPP, are largely used when referring to the organisation. The sources are unique being almost exclusively primary, consisting of mainly the notes, private papers and diary entries kept throughout the period. After the final chapter there is a list of background sources for further reference which takes the place of a bibliography. The issue of confidentiality is intended to be respected, and hopefully no one will be embarrassed or offended by the contents which are the perspectives of the author. The narrative of chapters 1–5 is really a plain man's history of a year by year, exciting and increasingly successful project. The final chapter is the hindsight of applied theology, showing the core philosophy for the author's private persuasion that the whole of life belongs to God as people understand Him, rather than to any exclusive belief system.

Acknowledgements

Although it may be invidious to mention individuals, I wish to put on record those people, without whose input in the first year, the project would not have got off the ground. From the outset, these were David Bedford of the Flora London Marathon, my wife Jean, Sohil Haj of Ibillin, Alan Pook of Brighton, John Sugden, Gary Stidder and Paul McNaught-Davies of the University of Brighton, Laurie Robinson of East Sussex, Alan Sefton of Arsenal Football Club, Atif Haj, Mayor of Ibillin, Auni Edris of Ibillin, Elias Haj of Ibillin, and His Excellency Francis Cornish and Mark Kelly of the British Embassy in Israel. After the initial success of July 2001, there were countless more splendid individuals, communities and organisations which are ever before me, notably the British Embassy, the British Council and the Israel Sports Authority. There will be even more in the future.

I have been fortunate in having a very patient wife who has, without complaint and only encouragement, allowed me to work at both the project and the writing of its story. In producing this material I have been indebted to those who have looked at parts, or all of the manuscript as it has gone through its various drafts. These allies have been Professor Paul Ballard, Eric Chandler, Dr Pat Dauncey, David Hallam MEP, Emma Jane Harper, Professor Larry Lerner, Professor Stephen Medcalf, Christine Murphy, Laurie Robinson, Jeanne Thomas MA, Professor Norman Vance, Brenda Vance MPhil, Ian Waller and Professor Haddon Willmer. I was also helped early on by the Very Rev. John Tidy, Dean of St George's Cathedral, Jerusalem, who kindly gave his experience and expertise. Gill and Ian Davis and Eric Evans gave great ideas about the production of the book. Vik Hill and Emma Varney have been invaluable with their patience, kindness and generosity as they facilitated an endless sequence of drafts. The loyal band of friends at Christ Church, Lewes, have been available with gifts I lacked and regularly needed, especially Peter Cane with his manuscript skills, Neil Fisher with his computer expertise, and the continuous encouragement of Dr David Smith and Professor Ken Smith.

The World Sports Peace Project

Geoffrey Whitfield and David Bedford met for lunch one day in 2000 to discuss World Sports and Peace. The outcome turned out to be astonishing. David said: "This could take off". And so the World Sports Peace Project began. It soon involved a network of contacts including government officials, embassy diplomats, civic leaders, communities, sports enthusiasts, schools and, above all, football playing youngsters and their parents in Israel.

The Galilee 2000–2003 project became a marker for community relations, with Arab and Jewish youngsters playing football together in their hundreds. It had a domino effect as excited youngsters returned home happily at the end of each day with remarkable stories to tell of friendships being made and mixed teams created. The result was a new dimension of optimism and energy for all who took part.

In the UK, scores of sports students from English universities, headed by the University of Brighton, gave up part of their summer vacation to assist. Student volunteers gave up the chance of paid vacation jobs and offered to work in the heat in Israel; the UK volunteer lists were over-subscribed. Various English organisations and Premier League clubs, most especially Arsenal, not only gave their support, but were involved in the equipping of the project.

At a time when there was bloodshed in other parts of Israel, in the Galilee there was a different kind of energy as young people learned to leave behind prejudices and to enjoy playing together in the same teams on the sacred turfs of football pitches.

Year on year, more and more Jewish and Arab communities wanted to be included and involved in the project. Other British organisations in the UK and Israel became fascinated and then drawn to participate in this rapidly developing project.

Elsewhere, people started to hear of the project and to take notice of such an unusual enterprise. They began to realise that they too could organise similar projects themselves. So they did, as the New Israel Fund and the Peres Center for Peace commenced initiatives elsewhere in Israel in 2005. In Palestine they assembled a group which wanted to do exactly the same thing. It will happen!

The idea could go anywhere in the world where there is conflict and division, because people can be brought together through sport. By playing on the same side they learn that when they play together as a team, they can go on to win. Even more importantly, they can find a different, enjoyable way of relating with each other, in this way replacing old animosities and divisions with concord and hilarious amity.

Abbreviations

ARIJ   Applied Research Institute – Jerusalem
BC   British Council
CCJ   Council of Christians and Jews
IOC   International Olympic Committee
IRCCI   Inter-Religious Co-ordinating Council in Israel
NIF   New Israel Fund
NGO   Non-Governmental Organisation
SCM   Student Christian Movement
SoP   Seeds of Peace
SSFP   Sussex Sport for Peace
UoB   University of Brighton
WSPP   World Sports Peace Project

This story is dedicated to

the host of unknown or scarcely seen people who
contributed to the project as private donors, supporters,
runners in the Flora London Marathon, coaches (and their
families) from the participant universities, encouragers
from churches, universities and organisations in
England, Israel and the West Bank.

Above all,
this book is dedicated to the wonderful
children and their families in the area of Galilee.

1

The Down to Earth Miracle, 2000–2003
and Thereafter

It was Highbury, the home of Arsenal Football Club, and it was 1 April 2004. The Bondholders Suite was being used by some 60 Israeli Jews and Arab Christians, Moslems, members of the Druze community, and members of UK universities. The date, with its associations, could not take away from the fact that a miracle was being experienced, which had its history of 'stepping stones' from 1993, culminating in that particular event. There had been more shootings, killings and acts of violence that same week between the communities in Israel and Palestine, just as in other parts of the world. But this particular group had spent their final day at Highbury, concluding five days together in a Training Camp Programme which had been largely conducted on the Eastbourne campus of the Chelsea School of Physical Education of the University of Brighton.

In the week before, they had prepared for an intensive, week-long Football/Conflict Prevention Project in Israel in July 2004. There, several hundred boys and girls, from families in 16 towns in Northern Israel, would play in mixed teams, Jew with Arab versus Jew with Arab. If a team was to win, Jews and Arabs would need to learn to trust and have confidence in each other, to work together and thereby gain the victory.

This 'miracle' became possible because of a three-year

1

programme which had earlier been created by World Sports Peace Project. It was conceived in 2000, shortly before the outbreak of the Second Intifada and continued thereafter, despite warnings of danger, and against a continuous background of charges of 'terrorism' and 'state terrorism'. Despite the issues of security becoming an increasing reality, the conduct of the projects never faltered, but rather continued to expand. Our presence at Highbury that day in April 2004, was because, from the early days of planning, Arsenal Football Club had been a significant player in supporting the project.

From 2000 onwards, communities in Israel were gradually brought together on an annual basis and very quickly the project grew, from 100 youngsters in Ibillin in 2001, to more than 300 from six towns in 2003. Moreover, it drew to itself, not only grassroot Arab and Jewish communities in Israel, but the involvement of the British Embassy, the British Council and the Israel Sports Authority. The participation of volunteers from one UK University in 2001, grew to include four universities in 2003. A UK coaching team of eight in 2001, became a group of 21 in 2003. And this was only the beginning.

The relevance of such a project could be clearly seen as Jewish and Arab children learned to feel less fearful of each other and more comfortable in each other's presence. To have in the same team, both Arabs and Jews who had to play together and find a spirit of confidence, has had significant effects both for the present and the future. It affected not merely the youngsters involved at the time, but the families to whom they returned each day, and their schools and peers.

This was not done in private, but was in the public domain, and towns had different factors to consider at such a time of tension. People who were fearful of each other were being introduced to a new factor: that people could find ways of being together and so replace their anxiety with confidence and trust. Towns could know ahead of time that their families would be having significant, close interaction of a positive and enjoyable nature which could continue year on year. This contrasted with the atmosphere of suspicion, fear and even hatred that existed in other communities which had not had this kind of opportunity. Those involved would never forget their first-hand experience. Indeed, they would tell their children and grandchildren of that time in their lives, and the consequences for their communities and societies.

So how could the first small project in 2001 change the face of a nation like Israel or any other nation? The answer is that it provided a three-year track record of a viable alternative to terrorism and violence which worked with the grassroots of communities and, with international connections, brought together the younger generation of families and communities. It provided a simple, constructive and pleasurable project so that the participants could experience the strength and commonsense of working creatively with a model, which they could see would be relevant to their social and political situation. Moreover it came to be recognised as such and was taken up by other organisations thereafter.

It was a powerful and dynamic alternative to the mistrust, misery, oppression and revenge in many parts of the land, where emotions were fanned by a cycle of vicious retaliation and blame. Such experiences, involving the mutilation and deaths of countless numbers, affected the fabric of each community which became threatened with fear and animosity. Each community had its history of horror stories, but had not yet become strong enough to move ahead to find solutions that would be viable for their children and grandchildren.

The philosophy behind the project had a theological base for some, but which did not need to be specifically expressed or emphasised because, invisibly, it was enshrined in its concept. The tradition of Christian humanitarian involvement goes back through the centuries, and one may easily look back to the English thinkers and reformers of the nineteenth century and pick out William Wilberforce, Charles Kingsley, Charles Dickens and many others. They combined with people of a range of different persuasions in order to achieve the success of their projects. This project would be part of that tradition of innovative involvement in the principles and practice of Conflict Prevention and Resolution in humanitarian terms, in which unspoken theological or political perspectives did not need to be spelt out. What created the teamwork was the unspoken agenda that the project was the right thing to do: that was the principle that the participants had in common, rather than holding to any more narrow formula. The project was quite simply a logical outcome of ordinary Christian belief.

The project first began with the idea of Conflict Resolution, but after meeting with Palestinians in Bethlehem in March 2002, it became clear that Resolution would be less necessary if, first, there was Conflict Prevention. The desire was to work with people from different faiths, as well as those without such allegiances. Nonetheless it was undeniable that the mainspring of the conception of the project although Christian in origin, did not need to be described, advertised or promoted as such. Therefore, not wishing to appear to have specific, religious designs as a project, the personal beliefs of individuals and communities were to be respected and not transgressed.

What follows is an account of how this was achieved, beginning with a dream and vision in 2000 until its completion as a three-year experiment in 2003. In the future, its track record of success and learning curves could be taken on by those who have the resources to develop it on a national and international scale. The second three-year period could see similar projects springing up throughout Israel, and possibly Palestine too. It was hoped that after 2003, the combined resources of the British Council and the Israel Sports Authority could extend the project in Israel and make it commonplace in the wider territory. Hopefully this will also be developed in the future with the appropriate authorities in Palestine.

The initiatives of volunteer coaches from the UK universities on an annual basis would be essential in building permanent alliances with local coaches from the communities. Together, these could create a structure whereby the programme becomes more than an annual event, but one that is established on a regular basis in the Arab and Jewish communities. This kind of project is for export, and can be translated into other sports and activities on a large scale. That is terrorism and conflict prevention; that is peace making on the ground, and that brings hope for a different future on a global scale.

The beginning of the Project – the move to bring Jewish and Arab youngsters together, April 2000

In 2000, Geoffrey Whitfield wrote his annual Easter letter to friends and in it asked for their support for work that had been going on in Israel and the West Bank since 1993. He told them about a youth club in Ibillin in the Galilee region of northern Israel, and a family therapy centre in Bethlehem. His visits were quite innocent, but nonetheless he was increasingly grilled by Israeli security at Ben-Gurion airport where he had to answer their questions about where he had been, and with whom he had associated. The mention of contact with Arabs and Arab communities, as well as Jewish friends and colleagues, led to serious, further questioning and long delays, before being permitted to continue with his journey. Being over 60 years of age, Geoffrey thought it quite comical, even gratifying, that he could be considered a threat to anyone, but the seriousness of his questioners could neither be doubted nor disputed, especially when they took his shoes for X-Ray inspection. However, with hindsight, it is evident that, without so intending, firm working relationships were being established with grassroots organisations. This was to be foundational for the work that was to come into being on a far larger scale. As the British Ambassador, His Excellency Sherard Cowper-Coles[1] was to say later at the Final Tournament in Israel in 2003: "From small acorns such as these . . . co-existence between Arabs and Jews comes about."

Every Easter, Geoffrey had raised funds for the Knights Youth Club in the village of Ibillin near Nazareth, which was organised by a group of local men and women, led by a teacher named Sohil Haj. It was distinctive because it was open to Arab Christian and Arab Moslem girls and boys, thereby breaking down two of the barriers in the society. In reply to the letter of Easter 2000, Alan Pook, a friend from Florence Road Baptist Church in Brighton, which they both attended, who was already a generous supporter of the Knights, phoned to offer some footballs for the club's summer camp. Alan was a great football enthusiast and very interested in youth development. It seemed such a natural extension of his gifts for him to see ahead to what might be a development in the skills of the young people in Israel. It was to become far greater than he ever realised, as his gifts were combined with the gifts of others, and a whole project grew from his initiative.

Shortly afterwards, he and Geoffrey shared the idea of taking football coaches in the future as well. It became clear that the existing summer camp could become swamped by football alone!

Alan's fertile imagination was also working because the next idea was to explore the possibility of having a separate football camp. Being aware of the delicate political nature of the land, Geoffrey realised that it was obvious that the football camp for the Knights could be extended from Israeli Arab Christian and Moslem youngsters to include Israeli Jewish youngsters. He knew that Sohil Haj also worked closely with Jews, and wanted to further the notion of grassroot, conjoint activities between the younger generations.

Soon it became apparent to Geoffrey that such a development in the Galilee region was something that could become national, even international. Both Geoffrey and Alan were clear that if youngsters could learn to play together as a team and work together for the same goal, they would be successful. This could be a practical reality, because children could put aside what divided them and find they had something in common, which could overcome their community divisions. This would have to have massive implications for the future of the country. The next step was to find ways to achieve that multi-dimensional objective.

As part of the process of turning ideas into a reality, Geoffrey and Jean took Alan, his wife Debbie and their youngest son Jack, to Ibillin in June 2000 for a weekend visit. Alan presented three footballs and some kit at a wonderful reception by the Club members and leaders. Geoffrey, Alan and the Knights' leaders then went on to discuss the foundations for a separate football camp the following Summer. The seeds were sown, and Alan went home richly satisfied.

The crucial nature of the project could only be realised if the proper connections were made with Jewish communities. Coincidentally, Sohil Haj had worked with a number of Jewish–Arab organisations and established bonds of colleague-ship in a number of areas. He was the man for the moment to make contacts that would be productive in the next phase. His voluntary role was critical in the formative stages of the project for the next three years. The conjunction of Geoffrey, Sohil and Alan was to be complemented by others very soon.

Before returning, Geoffrey had to continue the work he had been doing for a number of years and which had created the track record for being successfully involved in community projects with both Israeli and Palestinian professional care workers. With his wife Jean he moved on to Bethlehem to give further training to the local healthcare teams, and then south to Ashkelon hospital for the first of the staff training workshops in the specialist form of body psychotherapy, known as Bioenergetic Psychotherapy. These were hugely successful, and responded to with great enthusiasm. Anna Levi, the English therapist now resident with her family in Israel, had organised the sessions, after first planning them two years earlier in Jerusalem, and was delighted with the outcome. The workshops had nothing directly to do with the football project but it meant that Geoffrey became recognised as working with both Jewish and Arab communities in separate parts of the country.

The organisational beginnings and 12 months of planning for the next phase of development

Before leaving for their visit to Israel on June 6 the Chief Rabbi, Dr Jonathan Sacks, had spoken on the BBC Radio Four Today programme. He said that what people learn from the Holocaust is what happens when you do not treat people with dignity and Geoffrey wondered, at the time, to whom he was speaking. Was he speaking to the Israeli Knesset, or the Jewish Diaspora in the UK, or whom? Geoffrey felt sharply that this was a missing ingredient in all the talk of peace and resolved to meet Dr Sacks on his return.

That week, while he was in Israel and Palestine, Geoffrey was asking himself who were the people who could think on the large scale, at such a time in history as this. He did not need people with money, so much as those with a wide range of mind and heart. He felt there was the need to create a network of support from those who could introduce him to decision-makers who were also visionaries, and the face of a former student, David Bedford came to mind. David had been a world-record holder for a number of distances and was an Olympic Athlete in Munich in 1972 at 10,000 metres. Geoffrey and David had known each other when he was a student in Brighton in the late 1960s. They had not been in touch for many years, except around 1995 when Geoffrey had heard he was seriously ill and made contact with him, although by the time they spoke together, David had recovered. Nonetheless, the renewed contact had been warm and friendly. Geoffrey now phoned him again, and suggested they should meet and they met a few days later on 30 June 2000.

Over lunch, Geoffrey outlined the possibilities of a peace and sports project in Israel, through a football camp in Israel for youngsters from the divided communities. A tournament of mixed teams could be held and, as they learned to have confidence in each other and lose their distrust, they could turn themselves into winning teams and bring a new spirit to the area. Eventually this could develop into a global enterprise for sports people to take part in conflict prevention and resolution, by bringing together youngsters from divided communities anywhere in the world, and coaching them in team sports. David was silent, and then said four memorable words: "This could take off".

Neither of them was to know how far the conversation was to extend in range and significance within a very short time scale. They discussed the notion further and agreed to consider it in more detail over the summer. This led to a remarkable relationship over the next few years as there seemed to be an unspoken understanding between them about what could be done and what decisions could be implemented with the minimum fuss and the maximum efficiency. Geoffrey had been moved to contact David for his scale of mind. However, he had been remarkably out of touch with David's own development as a skilful leader, organiser and facilitator. Towards the end of the lunch, David mentioned to Geoffrey that the Flora London Marathon was the most successful fund-raising event in the country, with £25 million raised annually for charity by the event alone. Geoffrey had had no idea! "The steps of a good man are ordered by the Lord",[2] came to mind, and although he did not claim to be good, or to consider himself as such, he seemed to be directed by something much bigger than himself. They parted with a firm handshake, and a strong eye connection. They were on the move and it was to take them in a direction which neither of them could have foreseen.

Geoffrey and Jean had previously written in the 1990s to a number of Premier League football clubs and had kind responses from Glenn Hoddle, then manager of Chelsea, Kevin Keegan, then manager of Newcastle United and Bruce Rioch, then manager of Arsenal, all of whom gave encouraging responses, sending club pennants and photographs to the Knights Club in Ibillin. With the new development involving Jewish youngsters, they wrote again and Chelsea and Arsenal again responded, as did Middlesbrough, and Everton sent a football as a warm token of support. The involvement of Arsenal Football Club had only just begun and was to grow. The significance of these gifts was far-reaching, as English football clubs were, and still are, highly thought of in Israel by both Arabs and Jews. The impact on the youngsters in the Knights when they were presented with the gifts sent a current of energy through the members, and their clubroom was quickly decorated with them.

Contact was later made with the Brighton Evening Argus newspaper and BBC Southern Sound Radio, who also gave words of support. On July 3, Geoffrey wrote to a small group of individuals, whom he knew would have the same large scale of mindset, and asked them for their minds and hearts, not their money. Some came through with immediate support and ideas, so here was the immediate beginning of the network, which was to lead to the formation of a successful Working Group.

In September, David and Geoffrey met again, having given the idea greater thought. Both knew that they needed to think strategically and to find an organisation, sufficiently large, which had the resources to take the project on and extend it. They could do it themselves for a short period, perhaps three years, but they could not do it on a long-term basis. Was it to be the Save the Children Fund or the United Nations or another such organisation? Which one?

Over the summer months, they had considered the possible vehicles for the project. David asked if Geoffrey had seen the TV programme or read the book *One Day in September*. Geoffrey had indeed seen the programme, which was based on the 1972 Olympic Games in Munich, in which David had been a competitor. He had been moved by the way it sought to show the two sides, i.e. the desperate conditions of the Palestinian 'freedom fighters', or 'terrorists', and the similarly desperate situation of the murdered Israelis and their families. David had considered the matter, and come to the conclusion that the International Olympic Committee (IOC) might not only desire, but be able to handle the entire operation of global peacemaking through sport. It seemed so obvious!

Geoffrey proceeded with the daily running and extension of the project, having continuous interaction with David, who was operating in a private capacity. It was to become a fruitful relationship; there was no bank account, and no income, and any expenditure that was to be made came from their own resources. Geoffrey made contact with Ben Cohen who made the TV programme, and Simon Reeve, the author, and they were immediately supportive and encouraging. The name of Ankie Spitzer came to mind as essential to the process, as her husband, the fencing expert, had been killed in Munich at the 1972 Olympics, the details of which were included in the book and television programme, *One Day in September*.

At the same time links were being explored with Jewish leaders who might prove pivotal as decision makers. Following the words of the Chief Rabbi on the BBC Radio Four Today programme in June, Geoffrey wrote to him and suggested that they should meet. The Chief Rabbi's office contacted him and suggested that he should meet one of his Jewish cabinet ministers in London, Rabbi Barry Marcus. They met on July 25 at the Central London Synagogue. He transpired to be a man of passion and concern. He gave an incisive insight into the behaviour of the Israeli government, as well as its commitment to the Jews having the responsibility to be 'the Light to the Nations'. He was additionally impressed with Geoffrey's ideas of a project for Arab and Jewish children in Israel itself. He had a fervent wish for similar projects, and this item he felt was critical, in order to separate the difference between those who used words, and those who took action that was both relevant and enduring.

Within the hour, Rabbi Marcus linked Geoffrey to some far-seeing, key Jewish leaders. Brian Cohen, the Chief Executive of the British–Israel Chamber of Commerce was most informative, and willing to make connections. He, in turn, led him to the New Israel Fund (NIF), and their connections. Rabbi Marcus further encouraged him to meet Rabbi Malcolm Wiseman, and also the Council of Christians and Jews (CCJ). Contacts were later made with the Israeli Embassy and two diplomats, Ahuva Orem and Eli Yerushalmi. All were positive and forward thinking.

By 11 October 2000, the NIF in London had introduced him to

the New Israel Fund in Jerusalem which became far-reaching. Not only was there a meeting of hearts and minds, but in 2004 the NIF initiated their own project in Israel which was focused on the issue of racism and division in football. Later that day, Geoffrey and David had lunch with Alan Pook near Waterloo Station, and they set up the Sussex Sport For Peace organisation, the precursor to World Sports Peace Project. At the time the Intifada was breaking out in Israel and the West Bank, and shootings, stone-throwing and killings were in abundance in the Palestinian areas. It seems ironic that, at such a time as this, three Englishmen – Geoffrey, David, and Alan – were planning for peace. Alan felt he wanted to raise a team of runners in the Flora London Marathon to cover the costs of the project. Furthermore he planned to raise and lead a team of volunteer football coaches from Sussex. Two months later, by December 2000, it seemed that many matters had been sufficiently clarified for the three to meet again, and to put the project on a more formal footing.[3]

Meanwhile, on October 24, Rabbi Malcolm Wiseman visited Geoffrey at home in Ferring, West Sussex, and told him about an organisation called the Three Faiths Forum in the UK, and suggested a meeting with Rabbi Ron Kronish of the Inter-Religious Co-ordinating Council in Israel (IRCCI) when he next visited Israel. In order to find sports-minded people who might be interested in such a project, on November 6 Geoffrey visited the principal of Spurgeons College in London, Rev Dr Nigel Wright, for possible volunteers. He was supportive of the project, and agreed to let it be known to his students. It was surprising to Geoffrey that, in fact, none of the students, who were being trained for Christian ministry, came forward as volunteers. He had anticipated that he would be inundated with volunteers from the college, who would jump at the opportunity. It was not to be. Although it was disappointing, it was not uncommon for people to be enthusiastic, but unable to be more than encouraging because of their other commitments.

The same afternoon Geoffrey visited the offices of The Council of Christians and Jews in London, whose staff were very willing to help, and provide experience and expertise. A number of doors were opening, and those at the entrance were being taken aback at the coincidences or, in religious terms, even the mysterious working of God. While there was very little forthcoming in tangible terms of money, the project was becoming well-known, and receiving great encouragement and goodwill.

There had still been no meeting with the Chief Rabbi, but when the appointment was finally arranged for November 14, Geoffrey went with high expectations of a man who had spoken so movingly of dignity in relation to the Holocaust. Dr Sacks showed his interest in the subject, speaking freely of attending Arsenal matches at Highbury with the Archbishop of Canterbury. At the end of their discussions, after he had listened to the outline of the project, Jonathan Sacks said very simply: "Do it". Geoffrey had explained that he wanted not money, but people with a large scale of mind, and range of vision at such a time as this, because not everyone was ready to respond to this notion. Later on the same day, he met two diplomats at the Israeli Embassy and received great courtesy. However, the day had not been that simple, but instead, somewhat unnerving and uncomfortable. To gain entrance to both the Chief Rabbi and the Embassy, he had to pass through a new kind of experience - international security. The staff inside were very pleasant, but the questioning and the scrutiny, in between moving from one secure area to another before eventually gaining access, was hitherto quite unknown and out of experience. It was an introduction to a different world of danger.

Developing the network involved endless correspondence, travel and meetings, but the response was rarely anything other than immediate encouragement. The next visit by Geoffrey to Israel and the West Bank at the end of November 2000 was dramatic because it was a very dangerous experience, due to the inter-communal hostile reaction surrounding the second Al Aqsa Intifada. Both sides were in a state of fear. The hotels in Jerusalem were empty, and so were the flights. He was the only person in the Notre Dame Hotel in Jerusalem, whereas before there had been hundreds of guests. Despite the difficulties it was essential nonetheless, to sustain the training and therapy work in the West Bank in Bethlehem, then in Jerusalem and Ashkelon hospital.

While in Bethlehem he visited the home of an Arab lady whose house had been destroyed by Israeli incendiary gunfire, and those who went to put out the blaze had been fired on in turn. In the ruins of the building, Geoffrey surprisingly bumped into an English Member of Parliament who turned out to be Rt Hon

Donald Anderson, the Chairman of the Foreign Affairs Committee. This led to a positive communication between the two, which was very reinforcing for the project as it was becoming ever more widely known, despite the unpromising circumstances.

During the visit he contacted leaders of the Inter-Religious Council and the New Israel Fund. The NIF leadership in Jerusalem was very cautious, unlike their counterparts in London who had been extremely warm and enthusiastic. However as the morning wore on, more people came into the room to hear about the proposed project until a lively exchange had been established. Somewhat surprisingly, but much like what had previously been experienced, that warmth did not produce much that was tangible and the NIF and IRCCI did not provide resources of any kind. Nonetheless the warmth of contact was real and affirming and in 2004 the NIF mounted their own project on a large platform of inter-communal sport which attracted people from many parts of Europe. This included the leadership of the newly formed Football 4 Peace (F4P) which had been entrusted with the future of the WSPP in September 2003.

The practice of establishing a network of information and respect was continued in Israel and the UK over the months so that bridges of confidence and trust were established and reinforced. There was some astonishment, even incredulity, that at such a time an unknown group of people from Britain were planning to go there when there was fighting and bloodshed in so many places. But it was to lead to more expansive thinking in due course, especially with the NIF. Most meaningful of all, however, was the meeting with Ankie Spitzer, later Ankie Reches. After huge communication difficulties at first, the Israel Olympic Committee made it possible for her to know of Geoffrey's quest to meet her. This did eventually happen because she was evidently moved at his continuous faxes to the Israeli Olympic office seeking a meeting with her. Their encounter in a Tel Aviv café was rich in substance and emotion as they exchanged stories and experiences. He left with high hopes of a fertile peace-making process together. She gave him the name of the Abraham Fund, which supported the kind of project that was being planned but, although it was responsive and encouraging, there was no actual input or meeting. The project was, for many, premature for those who felt they were enduring a threat to their security, and here was a group from England reckoning on children from the two sides playing football together!

The beginnings of an effective working structure

On Geoffrey's return to the UK it was agreed that he, David and Alan should expand into a Working Group and include those who could advance the project for the following summer. On 21 December 2000, the first meeting of the Working Group took place at the Flora London Marathon offices. There were two issues being considered. Geoffrey, David Bedford and Alan Pook had already met on October 11, and worked out the local Ibillin football scheme. This was to be separate from a possible, more global, Olympic scheme, but the one could lead to the other and hopefully there would follow both the Olympic and Israeli/Palestinian thrust.

Alan Pook hoped to raise the funds from runners in the next Flora London Marathon in order to send the proposed ten football coaches from Sussex. He was confident that he could raise £20,000 to cover the costs of the project, due to his many sporting contacts. Much of this had been worked out, weeks earlier, and these ideas were outlined in a draft prepared by Geoffrey for the meeting. They decided to make a separate approach to the IOC for them to institute a non-political department, or sub-organisation, dedicated to peace in areas of conflict, attempting to bring peace within divided communities. This meant asking the IOC, who had the funds and personnel, to take up the organisation and management of sports projects at a global level, following the Sussex Sport for Peace (SSFP) initiative. It was felt that the project could be linked to the disaster of the 1972 Olympic Games in Munich, and be used as a memorial and springboard to all sides who had suffered the disastrous consequences, friend and foe alike. They knew that they would need to make contacts with those who could bring this to the IOC, and that also meant finding a unique and distinctive gap in the existing IOC organisation into which their project could naturally slot without issues of duplication arising. This intention was ambitious from the outset.

Meanwhile, planning for the first project in 2001 with the SSFP project was also under way. It was envisaged as a week-long football coaching/tournament event, conducted by football coaches from Sussex on a voluntary basis. It would be for boys and girls aged from 11–15 from the Jewish, Moslem and Christian communities from the grass root organisations in the villages of Ibillin and Misgav. This would be a completely separate module from the IOC approach, and would not be dependent on the success of the IOC. It would be a forerunner of what could become an annual event, and hopefully develop into the separate global scheme covering different sports for all nations, organised by the IOC. In the meantime the early funding would be achieved by volunteers running in the Flora London Marathon on 22 April 2001.

Progress was being made with the twin approach. Positive contacts had been firmly established with the New Israel Fund in the UK and Israel, the Council of Christians and Jews (CCJ) in the UK, the Three Faiths Forum in the UK and its counterpart in Israel, the Inter-Religious Co-ordinating Council in Israel (IRCCI). Moreover, positive encouragement had been given by the Chief Rabbi of the UK, Dr Jonathan Sacks. They had the interest of the Israel Olympic Committee, and the support and encouragement of the widow of Andre Spitzer, Mrs Ankie Reches. A meeting had been held at the Israeli Embassy with two ministers for Cultural and Public Affairs who were also very supportive of the scheme. At a local level, the marketing consultant for Lewes Town Hall, in East Sussex, had offered her services free to assist with publicity.

The Working Group on December 21, attended by Geoffrey, David, Alan and Jane Clements of the CCJ, was a very task-centred meeting. The exchanges took place with a sense of focus on openness of heart and hand, rather than any hierarchy, and so an informal process for the future conduct of business became established whereby mutual interchange took place until an agreement was reached. They discussed the way things had progressed regarding the project in Ibillin.

Alan gave assurances about the raising of funds, via runners in the Flora London Marathon that April, with special support from Dorothy Stringer School in Brighton and the Legal & General Insurance Company office in Brighton. He also outlined the project itself which should not only be cross-cultural, but inclusive of both genders. Accommodation and local support was an issue, and it was agreed that there should be one central venue for staff and for the games themselves, rather than dispersed venues. Moreover, every participant should have a memento, and not just the winners. His main contact in Ibillin would be Sohil Haj, who was the leader of the Knights Youth Club, with whom he had already met and exchanged ideas.

The possible global project, with Olympic Aid, presented work for the Working Group that needed to be done, for which there were no guidelines, and these had to be created rather rapidly. This included finding a distinctive slot which could fit into the existing IOC programme, so that it was not involved in any duplication of projects. As the IOC worked through national organisations, it meant that any project could be politically sensitive. Therefore, even though the plan was to work in Israel, it might be necessary to consider offering to conduct a project in a less emotive area. This indicated the need to have some demarcation between what was envisaged in Israel with the local Sussex project, and something eventually more global with the Olympic connection. Jane Clements of CCJ willingly offered logistical support from her contacts in Israel for that particular emphasis.

The group separated the tasks and divided the responsibilities amicably. In the future arrangements, David Bedford saw himself as one who would help in a private capacity, being reactive and supportive to the scheme's management and needs. He could liaise with Geoffrey and Alan as the structure developed, and identify ways of proceeding with and developing the tasks. Alan would be responsible for the SSFP tournament, and seeing through the arrangements with the various personnel involved in fund-raising for travel, equipment, accommodation and the supply of coaches. Jane would offer fundamental advice to ensure the proper connections were made, and to provide information on resources. Geoffrey would continue to act as co-ordinator of the whole project, proactively initiating and developing further contacts for the network. This creating and sustaining of relationships meant that individuals and organisations were kept regularly informed and updated, so that they felt included and important to the operation.

The structure that emerged was one that was informal, based on a mutual understanding of what needed to be done and a commitment to do it. There was no quest for control or authority, but instead the unspoken agreement to press ahead with the tasks at hand. The atmosphere was created by a meeting of colleagues, who, in their own right, were expert leaders, in which no one sought to exert authority over the others. The power to move ahead was vested in the small group, rather than any one individual or organisation. The drives and rewards were neither financial nor material, but simply the recognition of the primary task, with the intention to see the work completed in the short term. In the long term, they knew that the consequences could have far-reaching effects in Israel and Palestine, and anywhere in the world.

In summary, by Christmas 2000, the work seemed well in hand for the summer football project in Ibillin, and the meeting moved on to begin to clarify the next steps for the larger project. It was also clear that the next phase was to find people who could enable them to meet the IOC. David suggested that Craig Reedie could be the person, as he was the UK representative and he arranged a date for him to meet with Geoffrey and himself in London on 16 January 2001. Things were decisively moving ahead.

January 2001 was a pivotal month. On January 4 Geoffrey went to London, at the suggestion of Rabbi Ron Kronish of IRCCI in Jerusalem, to meet with Sir Sidney Sternberg, the Chairman of The Three Faiths Forum in the UK. The first step was to meet the secretary, Sidney Shipton, who was to make the arrangements for the second meeting. He was able and willing to give his time to attend the Working Group, but was limited in what he could deliver of substance to the project. Moreover, the intended meeting between Geoffrey and Sir Sidney Sternberg was never put in place. However, the group had been joined by Laurie Robinson, a management consultant from East Sussex, whose expertise and enthusiastic input was invaluable throughout. The contrast was perhaps more an example of the learning curve for the Working Group itself, as it endeavoured to find the kind of people who could make a creative difference to the progress of the project and its vision.

On the same day Geoffrey made contact with others concerned with Israel and Palestine at a meeting held at St Mary's College near Twickenham, by an organisation called "Living Stones" which was particularly involved in Israel and Palestine. The most significant event for him that day came from a casual conversation in the afternoon with Sir Harold Walker, President of Care International, who had been the UK ambassador to Syria, and was therefore acutely aware of the situation throughout the Middle East. He gave Geoffrey two significant extensions to the network and, in particular, the name of William Morris, Secretary General of the Next Century Foundation, who was later to prove a solid and remarkable resource for networking and insight. Sir Harold also gave the name of a Moslem contact in London, Nadeem Kazmi, a lawyer, from the al-Khoei Foundation, and he and Geoffrey met a few weeks later at Gatwick airport in February. He, too, was very informative and helpful, though also somewhat cautious about a project, as yet unproven.

Early contact with the Olympic movement

Another most significant event of January 2001 was the meeting a week later at the London Hilton Hotel between Geoffrey, David Bedford and Craig Reedie. Craig was the UK representative on the IOC, a Scottish lawyer and a very constructive, well-informed person. David and Geoffrey introduced the notion of the global project, and Craig immediately grasped the point, and moved straight into being proactive. He suggested people in the procedural ladder, a Norwegian, Johann Olav Koss, the director of Olympic Aid, and two others involved in the Olympic Committee. Craig asked them for their statement of intent, and Geoffrey provided the following concise, sharply focused paper for him within 48 hours:

INITIAL CONCEPT – DRAFT

"Wherever in the world there is a need for conflict resolution, a culture of mutual trust has to be created to displace that of suspicion and alienation.

Projects need to be put in place so that people from differing communities find practical ways of finding this to be an authentic possibility. Sport is the ideal means of bringing divided people together. Team sports events, and their associated training, are ideally suited to create trust through teamwork in troubled areas

18

and can act as a mobilising force to neutralise the destructive atti-
tudes of the world in which divided people live.

The Olympic movement is uniquely placed to promote global
schemes on an ongoing basis, where personnel and funds are made
available, with sports ventures so organised that, in areas of divi-
sion, there could be sown a different dimension and culture.

A pilot project of the above concept is to be held in July 2001 in
northern Israel, organised by Sussex Sport For Peace and the
Knights Youth Club in Ibillin. This will compose of youngsters
aged 11–15 from the three communities, Jew, Moslem and
Christian. They will be coached by a team of football coaches from
Sussex, England, for one week. It will conclude with a tourna-
ment, with each team consisting of members from the three
communities.

The wider vision could be that similar sports schemes across the
world are organised and sustained in areas of similar conflict. The
results should be self-evident. The consequences for the partici-
pants and their communities represent hope for the future on a
scale that is global."

Craig Reedie responded before nightfall the same day. The
evening before, he had met Johann Olav Koss in London and
immediately discussed the project. The project had taken several
steps further in just a few hours. Their statement of intent led to
the title, 'World Sports Peace Project', in order to show that the
extent of their concern stretched beyond Sussex and Israel.

The next Working Group meeting took place in late February.
It had become clear that the Ibillin project was a pathfinder, and
that future projects could lie in other parts of the world beyond
Israel and Palestine. Thus there were options to work globally
with the Olympic movement, via Olympic Aid, as well as the
proposed project in Israel for Arabs and Jews which itself seemed
unique and distinctive. The network of contacts in the UK and
Israel was already extensive and still spreading further. The
Working Group was also growing and moving ahead.

This Group was also notable for decision making. It was
agreed to arrange a meeting with Johann Olav Koss, Director of
Olympic Aid, who lived in Canada, but who passed through
London from time to time. This was essential if there was to be
mutual understanding and appreciation of each other's work,

and to ensure whether it would be possible to be mutually involved in global ventures together.

Separately, much still rested on the progress on the football side of the project, and with the fund raising. In the absence of Alan Pook, a number of critical matters were raised so that he could give updates for discussion at the next meeting in March. These included ensuring that the local people in Israel were clear about their own organisation, leadership and responsibility for control and resources. The details needed to be put in writing by them so that, in London, there was no mistake about the dates, venues, schools and bodies that would be involved, including the equipment, pitches, balls, nets, goalposts and all the other logistics. The Working Group needed to be assured that they would have a team of leaders able to take responsibility for different factors. A clear timetable was needed, covering events for each day of the week, and including educational activity in order to discuss subjects about community relationships. It was quite a long list, but at such a distance the liaison between the UK and Israel could not be left to chance.

Jane Clements reported that transport and accommodation for the coaches in Israel should present no problem. It was anticipated that the project would seek support for the camp with visitors like Ankie Reches. It was clear to the Working Group that Alan Pook and his coaching team should be fully supported to ensure a successful outcome to the camp so that it continued in future years and was seen to be a landmark venture for the future.

Within two weeks of the Working Group meeting, Geoffrey, David and Johann Olav Koss met early on Sunday morning, March 4, at London-Heathrow. Johann made clear that he was cautious about work in Israel, but was supportive of the plans nonetheless. Discussion followed about whether, and how, the English project could blend its work together in the future after 2002. Was it to be an application from the English side to Olympic Aid, or for Olympic Aid to recognise the English project, and then to become mutually combined?

Olympic Aid had firm criteria for their work in the different countries, with aims, objectives and evaluation processes clearly documented. It was made clear to Johann that Olympic Aid would be very welcome to visit the football camp and to have hands-on experience of the work. It was made equally clear by

Johann that the greatest success of the camp would be if it was held at all, when one contemplated the prevailing situation. If it was to be continued after 2001, that would be considered, but at that moment it was a one-off operation, although it soon became obvious that it would need to be a three-year project. The July football camp, meanwhile, was not dependent on the outcome of the contacts with Olympic Aid. One significant difference was that the volunteers at the camp would participate for one week only, and that was different in style to Olympic Aid who worked with volunteers doing a six-month commitment. Moreover, the participants from the UK would not be paid, and would generally be expected to cover their own costs.

Johann pointed out that the Working Group would need to document, in detail, the preparation for the camp, and to evaluate its development and week-long activity, with the results, as far as they were measurable. Everything should be carefully written up for the benefit of evaluation and presentation to Olympic Aid and other interested bodies. It was a strategic move forward, and Geoffrey felt this could be assisted by the School of Social Sciences from the University of Sussex, where he had once been a chaplain.

They discussed how it was essential to learn from the grass roots of Ibillin what they wanted, in both the short and long term, for their community. It was their needs that focused the task for the UK group, and not vice versa. It was recognised that the major problem in the area was not poverty so much as racism between the three communities, which presented a devastating cultural and lasting threat. The mutual respect and appreciation of each other's cultures through sport was of primary importance as a goal of the entire operation. This meant that some kind of educational programme could be included e.g. community and environmental issues.

It was a very creative meeting with good personal contact between the three, and much mutuality and agreement of understanding. Olympic Aid did not work in Israel and Palestine, and Johann Olav Koss was impressed by the UK initiatives. He was invited by Geoffrey to send someone from Olympic Aid to attend the project in July, and he was supportive of the idea. There was no discussion about any criteria for the role of that person, and, with hindsight, that was unfortunate and led to misunderstandings later. However, Sohil Haj in Israel and the Working Group in London were informed about the results of the successful Heathrow meeting, prior to the next Working Group. The preparation work had been going for a year and although plans were in abundance, no funds, youngsters or coaches were in place.

Early initiatives with the English Universities

The following week, Geoffrey made contact with old associates of the University of Sussex where he had been a chaplain thirty years earlier. Following the Olympic Aid suggestions for evaluation of the project, he needed to discuss research with the deans in the Schools of Afro-Asian Studies, and Cultural and Community Studies. Although this was warmly and sympathetically received, it was the contacts he made with the Chelsea School of Physical Education of the University of Brighton, where he had also been a chaplain, which produced the next sequence of events. Alan Tomlinson, their Head of Research, had been suggested as a knowledgeable person to guide them in terms of what might be possible. When they met in March, Alan swiftly saw the intentions and possibilities of the project, and the scope for the involvement of the university. As a senior member of staff, he suggested the name of Professor John Sugden, who, in the past, had been involved in sports projects in Northern Ireland in the 1980s. Although this had been a long time ago, and in a very different context, the idea seemed to have potential and so it was to prove.

By now, the project planning had been going on for almost one year, and much had been accomplished, yet much remained to be discovered and still more to be achieved. However, time was short as it was anticipated that there would be an Arab–Jewish Football/Conflict Prevention Project in only three months. The Working Group had done much groundwork, but they had more hope and expectations, plus the anticipation of more hard work rather than anything concrete. Those next three months were to be significant. Those who were eventually to join the project did not always realise the immense amount of time, effort and private expense that had been involved for a very few people. It took some time to appreciate that the project had its roots in years of initiative and work in the local area since 1993. There was a groundswell of goodwill, as well as caution, but the project now needed components, as well as structure, if it was to succeed.

Within the structure there were already some problems to be addressed and overcome. Because it had grown so successfully and speedily, Alan Pook was over-stretched and could not extend his focus on the project beyond his crucial initial enthusiasm for the football input in Ibillin. As it was essential that he had lieutenants in place to cover the work, he and Laurie Robinson met to find ways of working even more effectively. The Group had to find its own way of working, and without a 'manual', they were beginning to write their own.

A long list of questions was prepared for discussion at the Working Group meeting in March. They included essential items such as liaison so far with Sohil Haj regarding leadership, extra educational activities, detailed costs for local transport and travel in Israel. In the UK, there were other matters, including the Marathon runners and the collection of sponsorship money, precise equipment needs for the camp, the names of the football coaches and details of the training programme.

In turn, Sohil Haj and Jane Clements compiled another long list which included the number of children at the camp. They estimated about 150 children within the age group of 7–13, but along with this had to be included accommodation and timetables, meetings with the local Ibillin organisers and the exact dates for the camp. It was obvious that the idea of organising the project was far more complex and time consuming than had been originally imagined or understood. Following this, the situation became still more complicated, as the people involved had to adjust to new ways of working as a team, in a project where there was neither chart nor compass to guide them. The essential issue of research was also becoming difficult to work through. Earlier in the month, Geoffrey met the Dean of Afro-Asian Studies at Sussex University, Mick Johnson, to discuss how they might conduct quality research, and he, too, hoped to give help and advice. However, he later found that it would not be possible to conduct the research formally after all, because of lack of Middle East experts, although he still wished to help in other ways.

Financial accountability was also essential and Geoffrey

liaised with Bible Lands which, as a reputable and properly constituted registered charity, could administer the funds they raised. At the time it was perceived that their work in Ibillin since 1994 fitted in with the requirements of the Charity Commissioners. This continued to their great benefit, until a change of Bible Lands personnel and structure took place in 2003, and the arrangement was cordially concluded.

The inclusion of the University of Brighton and Arsenal Football Club at the end of the first year

In late March Geoffrey went to Eastbourne, and met Professor John Sugden for the first time. He grasped the point very quickly and was immediately keen, joining the Working Group a few days later. The Working Group meeting of March 28 was pivotal for a number of reasons. It was essential to recognise that the project had grown very quickly in a short space of time. By the time the University became involved there was the occasional mention of 'short notice' and 'being rushed for time'! All true for some, because they were to be in Israel four months later. However, the planning had been going on for a year, and it took time for them to realise that they were 'the new kids on the block'. But what 'new kids'! After the initial meeting with Alan Tomlinson, followed by the meeting with John Sugden, a team swiftly emerged. Gary Stidder, a senior lecturer, came on board to help choose the coaches and then to take responsibility for the coaching component in the summer. An unseen background team was in place, which included the backing of the Head of Department, Paul McNaught-Davis, assisted by Frances Powney. Doubtless there were other backroom people who combined to produce an effective taskforce.

It was necessary to begin to function as a body with account-able responsibility, rather than to act simply as individuals. Nonetheless, many exploratory initiatives would still need to be made, but within a formal framework. It needed to be understood that the project already had a track record of work in Israel that went back to 1993 and that it was not, therefore, without experi-ence and had established strong, grassroots relationships. Indeed another visit to Israel had already been arranged for early June to strengthen the contacts already made with the British Embassy and other official bodies.

The meeting confirmed a number of points. Geoffrey was given the temporary title of Official Co-ordinator of the project, and finances were to be formally handled by Bible Lands. Decisions would continue to be made in future by consensus within the Working Group. Laurie Robinson had presented a clear outline for the Summer project in Ibillin, with tasks to be performed and deadlines within them. However, the organisation of the fund-raising runners in the forthcoming Flora London Marathon still needed proper co-ordination. The Working Group agreed that everything needed to be fully in hand by the next meeting on May 1. John Sugden agreed to attend to the details of the research, but indicated that costs could be involved.

On 19 April 2001, Geoffrey went to Arsenal Football Club at Highbury, and met Alan Sefton who was in charge of their community football projects. A few weeks earlier in the match programme, Alan had given some details of his involvement in a football project close to Ibillin in Misgav in Northern Israel. He knew and understood the situation very well because he had been responsible for the project which brought together youngsters from the Jewish and Bedouin communities. Emma Jane Harper, the journalist, passed on her copy of the match programme to Geoffrey and he immediately made contact with Alan at Highbury. Alan was very creative, with many suggestions for the football programme, appreciating that this new project was on a larger scale, but far less financially supported. His knowledge and input were immensely important and he contributed footballs and cones from Arsenal, as well as personal expertise, on a regular basis thereafter. His generosity with his time and advice provided a reliable basis of resource and encouragement. Moreover, the sense that a club the size and status of Arsenal was prepared to be interested in such a small enterprise indicated its scale of competence and awareness. The project's connection with the prestigious Arsenal Football Club was a boost to the standing of the project in Israel. In the same way it was a boost for the project in the UK and those coming on board. To know that this initiative was considered worthy of support produced constructive results in terms of encouragement. More help came from Arsenal when extending hospitality to the

Misgav officials who came to the UK in the late Spring. There were football clubs who could also have become involved, and Arsenal's was a splendid example to others.

Meanwhile, however, there could be no project without a team of coaches, and the funds necessary to send them to the project in the Galilee. Only when this was accomplished, could any of the other plans of the previous 15 months be implemented. Then there would be a viable project. The project had come a long way in a short time and much had been learned and assimilated; enthusiasm was in abundance and skills were being tapped efficiently and effectively. A fine stream of communication between those involved meant that everyone was being updated and kept abreast of developments. At this point there was an integrity of purpose in the main players, with a task centredness that was focused on getting the work accomplished. So far, so good, but could the project be delivered?

2

The Turning Point for the First Project in 2001

The raising of the funds and the coaching team, April 2001

The raising of the funds through runners in the Flora London Marathon took place on 22 April 2001 with seven runners – three less than the ten originally promised. It was a learning curve for future organisational skills, as the project met hitches in many different ways, but overcame them. The money forthcoming for the project was seriously less than the £20,000 first promised, and less even than the later revised figure. There could be no spare money for a research project. Moreover, the collection of the sponsorship money proved surprisingly difficult and time consuming. We were coming to terms with the difference between enthusiasm and delivery.

Certainly, the seven who did the run were heroes, and every runner completed the course. Alan Pook had worked strenuously to fulfil that part of his commitment. Many will gladly volunteer for a task, especially if it has the cachet of 'running the London Marathon'. However not everyone carries through on a promise, including, sometimes, even an enthusiastic sponsor. There had to be many learning points for this in the future, despite the fact that Geoffrey wrote to every runner, both before and after the run, as well as meeting them personally two weeks before the Marathon itself.

The next meeting of the Working Group took place just over

one week later on May 1. At the suggestion of Jane Clements of the CCJ, the Working Group was attended by Steven Fine, the Chief Executive of the Maimonides Foundation. It was hoped that he would be able to liaise with the Jewish community in Misgav, but after initial enthusiasm, an effective delivery of services and resources did not materialise.

By the time of the Working Group in May, Geoffrey had taken on the organisation of the project as Alan Pook had become increasingly pressed for the time that the project required. He confirmed at the meeting that he would be unable to take the coaches to Israel, so the change in responsibility was timely. This must have been a very costly decision for Alan because he had helped to spark off the notion when he first offered some footballs, following Geoffrey's Easter appeal letter the previous year. His enthusiasm for the project had not waned, but he did not have available time to give. That was becoming increasingly necessary and demanding, as more detailed work needed to be done than had first been realised, which included increasing liaison with a growing number of other individuals and organisations.

The estimated funds from the Flora London Marathon were reduced again, and Alan reported that it would now possibly only raise in the region of £7,000. An estimate of costs was presented as being just over £6,000. Two years later the budget for 2003 was in excess of £30,000! Meanwhile, it had been ascertained that there would be no funds forthcoming from Olympic Aid to cover the costs of research, despite their request that there should be such a programme. It was agreed that a full report would nonetheless be prepared for possible research when the team was in Israel, and conducting the project.

On the positive side, it was reported that the University of Brighton was actively raising the mixed gender team of coaches for the coaching side of the project, as the team originally hoped for from the Brighton community was not forthcoming. A meeting with the potential coaching team from the University in Eastbourne was arranged, and would be briefed by Geoffrey and Jane Clements of CCJ.

It was agreed to ask Sohil Haj to ensure that a Jew and a Moslem should join him in making a strategic team of three, so that it could be seen that the project was working with those communities, with representation from each. This he achieved by the time of the meeting in May and it was agreed that Geoffrey should go to Ibillin at the end of May to meet those concerned, to ensure that everything was ready for July.

Logistical issues such as equipment, transportation and personnel, as well as the local programme in Ibillin, were also covered, and responsibility taken by individuals. Laurie Robinson produced a paper regarding future organisation, and formal registration as a charity. As a result, it was agreed that after July they would see how the project might be developed in conjunction with any other organisations in the same field. In the meantime, the Working Group agreed to work together in the spirit of good governance, as any other charitable or corporate organisation. Without so intending, it had emerged to become a Non-Governmental Organisation (NGO).

Contact with the British Embassy, the British Council, and the first Anglo–Arab–Jewish meetings

The final reconnaissance trip by Geoffrey took place between 31 May and 4 June 2001. Prior to this, a letter was sent to the principal people in the region to ensure that the meetings, which were already established, had a detailed, written checklist. This sought to cover everything from the Israeli side.

The visit began with a strategic and creative meeting with Mark Kelly, the First Secretary of the British Embassy, at the Commodore Hotel in Tel Aviv. Geoffrey had foreseen that a formal relationship needed to be properly established with the Embassy so that they were fully informed about the project and its intentions. Equally it meant that the team from the UK was properly advised. This would avoid any possible misunderstanding about the arrival in the country of a group of unknown Britons, however well intended. Geoffrey briefed him with details of the project so that the Embassy officials should know of their intentions in the country and thereafter. Mark Kelly responded positively and creatively, particularly to the request that the British Ambassador, His Excellency Francis Cornish, should present the trophies and medals on the final day of the tournament. It was, strategically, a most important arrangement in what had been a constructive and timely encounter.

However, the following night brought another chilling and sobering experience. The night club, situated only a short distance from the hotel, was bombed with serious loss of life. It was clear that the timing of the project was appropriate at such a time as this, when there was destruction of both lives and trust between the communities. The project was a symbol of hope for the future at a time when morale was low, and fear and rage very high on the agendas of people from both communities. It was critical, therefore, for the project to go ahead, and not to withdraw, although that was the natural expectation of the Israelis.

During the visit, telephone contact was established with the British Council offices in Tel Aviv, West Jerusalem, East Jerusalem, and Nazareth, especially with Caron Sethill who was in a senior position in the West Jerusalem office. As with the British Embassy, it seemed not only correct but, likewise, strategically essential to make formal contact, in order that they too should be informed of the forthcoming project, and the visit of a number of British visitors. The responses were courteous at first, though somewhat quizzical, but became increasingly and significantly helpful. The arrangement was made with the British Council that, in July, their office in Nazareth would receive the consignment of football equipment from the UK, via David Bedford, and that it could be collected on the first day after arrival. It was the beginning of a fertile relationship which no one could have anticipated at the time.

The meetings in Ibillin over the weekend were successful, despite many obstacles needing to be overcome. Happily, representatives from the three communities were present. There was an indication that one or two wanted to know if they personally would receive anything from the project, and Geoffrey had to make clear that no one was to be paid for their involvement, either from the UK or locally. The Jewish representative from the community in Misgav was very enthusiastic and promised the supply of a minibus throughout the project to assist in transportation.

The major problem at the time centred on the availability of the football pitch which had been promised the previous year. If a satisfactory pitch could not be made available, there could be no project. The UK team had no idea of what was going on behind the scenes and it seemed strange that the issue had not been resolved long in advance. It was the first of many mysteries, some of which were never fully understood. Every summer the problem of the availability of the pitch in Ibillin arose, and each year the UK team had to make clear that if there was no pitch, there could be no coaching team or tournament. Later, Geoffrey made clear in conversation and in writing that, if the football pitch that had been promised was withdrawn, it would not be possible to recommend the project to the Working Group in London. Possibly, it took a great deal of effort behind the scenes to bring about the eventual use of the football pitch, and some unknown people were much appreciated! The local complications were overcome, and the Ibillin sports director, Auni Edris, became increasingly proactive and provided a very acceptable set of resources, without which the project could not have been held.

It also became apparent that there were significant differences within each individual community, which pointed to unresolved differences over the years. Communication between the communities could be very complicated, and was not always easily overcome because of their outstanding internal issues. It could happen that one set of representatives could attend a meeting and give assurances which would not necessarily be carried through, because different people from the same community did not agree for a variety of (often unknown) reasons.

In summary, Geoffrey was able to assure the Ibillin and Misgav groups that the UK would provide the coaches and the equipment, if they provided the pitch and the children. Although it was to be in the school holidays, each community, Jew, Christian and Moslem, agreed to provide one third of the children, aged from 9 to 14. The grassroots partners agreed to ensure that there would be an adequate football pitch, and that meals, accommodation and transport would be provided. They would also see to the Social Education/Conflict Resolution half of the project. Optimism was in the air, although tinged with some doubts too! It was all quite new for everyone involved but there was a pioneering spirit that the project would be carried through, whatever difficulties arose. Sohil Haj was able to say: "All our objectives have been achieved". We were on course, although there was still much to be done.

On Geoffrey's return, John Sugden was in touch to say that the University of Brighton had agreed that Patrick Johnson, a research student doing an MA in Conflict Resolution through Sport, was to be seconded to the programme. This encouraging news meant the project was to obtain the research it required, without charge to its slim funds.

At the Working Group meeting on 11 June, Gary Stidder, a senior lecturer, and Patrick Johnson, both of the University of Brighton were introduced and a number of key decisions made. These decisions resulted in Geoffrey having overall responsibility for the project, with Gary Stidder as the hands-on organiser of the coaching side, and Patrick Johnson pursuing the research. David Bedford undertook responsibility for the collection and transportation of the equipment, including the substantial gift of 60 footballs and 50 marker cones donated by Arsenal FC illustrating their ongoing commitment to the project. Alan Pook undertook to ensure the delivery of the funds from the Marathon, which he hoped would amount to £7,000. Around £5,000 was eventually forthcoming, which covered the major expenses, but left a gap still to be filled.

Final arrangements were made with Gary to ensure that six selected coaches would travel with him on July 27. Patrick Johnson and Steven Fine would travel two days earlier, on the 25th, to ensure everything that had been promised was in place. Steven agreed to ensure the provision of nine bedroom fans from Misgav. Eventually, these were not forthcoming because of the late withdrawal of the Misgav community and they were provided by the guest-house. Equally the promised minibus from Misgav was not to be made available for the team. Separately, Steven reported that the Mayor of Misgav, Erez Kreisler, was to visit Arsenal FC at Highbury on June 28, and asked Geoffrey and Gary to be present. This was agreed, and Patrick Johnson was also included for the meeting.

It was confirmed that Ibillin would take care of the provision of transportation from the airport, and provide accommodation and hospitality. They had also managed to ensure the provision of the grassed football pitch after all. The educational/social activities were to be conducted locally by experienced people. The project would cover the cost of equipment and transportation, bed and breakfast guest-house accommodation, and flights, except for Gary and Patrick who were covered by the university. These commitments, at both the university and the personal level, gave clear evidence of the engagement of the institution and the individuals taking part. Each member of the coaching team was giving their time and professional skill without remuneration. Already it had become clear that financially, it was to be a close run thing, and the generosity of them all was to be one more pivotal point in enabling the project to go ahead. It was a sign of her commitment that one of the coaches, Emma Day, quietly undertook to cover all her expenses, which was also a symbol of the vision that most people carried around with them and put into effect.

On June 15, Geoffrey went with Jane Clements to the University of Brighton at their Eastbourne campus to meet the six coaches with Gary and Patrick, and to give a briefing on expectations and the nature of the community in Ibillin. The coaches were very motivated and looked a magnificent team. When Geoffrey thanked them for their willingness to commit themselves, one of the coaches, speaking for them all, said that it was they who wished to thank him for the opportunity of joining such a project.

On June 28, one month before the project was to commence, a meeting was held at Highbury with the Mayor of Misgav, Erez Kreisler where a variety of issues were raised and discussed. It was a very important meeting because Arsenal had already been supportive of a football experiment with youngsters from the region and a Bedouin village. Alan Sefton of Arsenal had sustained a good relationship with the community and he confirmed the promise of footballs for the tournament. The Mayor, Erez Kreisler, confirmed the agreement with his Director of Football on June 3, and gave assurance that, while there could be hitches because of the time of the year, they would daily send a team of 50 children, plus two assistant coaches from Misgav. Moreover he would see to the provision of accompanying school teachers, and ensure that the children each carried their refreshment bag. He also addressed the issue of local publicity, and Steven was to liaise with Misgav and Ibillin on the subject. The mayor also raised the matter of success and failure and Geoffrey impressed on him the need to discern between failure and the notion of 'find and discover faults as part of a learning curve'. What mattered was to prepare as meticulously as possible, work as hard as possible, and to experience and learn. If the project took place, that would be a remarkable success, as well as a great beginning for future enterprises. Everything seemed in good order and the summer project was knitting together and looked promising.

By late June, Geoffrey had successfully written to a number of friends, soliciting around £1,000 in financial support, in case of a shortfall in money raised by the Marathon runners. Although Marathon money eventually reached a total of around £5,000, it was short of the £6,000 that was needed, and it was a close run thing!

Last-minute hitches!

However on July 3 Sohil phoned Geoffrey from Israel to say that the Misgav contingent suddenly wanted to have armed security guards for their children on the coaches, and at the stadium. He had to make it clear that what Misgav did in terms of transportation was their affair, but WSPP could not agree to any armed presence in the stadium. Moreover, the subject had at no time been raised for proper discussion in their meetings. The greatest disappointment came in mid-July with less than two weeks to go: Misgav pulled out of the arrangements, despite the assurances given on June 3 and June 28 by their senior officials. The reasons defied logic and it appeared that they simply could not admit that something had gone wrong internally and resorted to blaming others, e.g. they had not had enough notice, they had not been able to contact anyone, and it was the school holidays. A Jewish friend said later: "Someone led you up the garden path and you'll never know why".

There was another serious hitch, which, from the Nazareth office, concerned the sports equipment from the UK. Jane Shurrush of the British Council informed Geoffrey that the Israeli customs would not release the equipment, even though it was designated to go to their official office in Nazareth. Moreover, the department asserted that they did not know the address of the office, even though it was in the grounds of the hospital which had been in the town for decades. It was the first of the annual problems with different Israeli officials about the delivery of the equipment. On Monday July 23 the project was still unsure if the

34

equipment would be delivered and yet the team was due to leave on Friday the 27th. Finally it arrived, but not without some serious hard work by Jane Shurrush, who had been increasingly astonished at the intransigence of the officials.

A temporary encouragement was the news from Olympic Aid on July 18, nine days before departure, who agreed to send an observer/researcher, Michelle Donnelly, from Canada. Being delighted with the news, no enquiries were made about her background, role and responsibility, nor were boundaries laid down, either by the Working Group or Olympic Aid. The relationship eventually became somewhat difficult between her and other members of the team, which was a disappointment. There would always be complexities in any team mixture, and although it did not interrupt the flow of the project, it was to be another important learning experience about team building. It was also realised, days after the arrival in Israel, that they had sent a Jewish lady. Too late, either a Jew or an Arab would have been declined at such a sensitive time. It was hardly fair for either organisation to reckon to place anyone from that background in such a role without careful preparation and understanding. Inevitably there would be different perceptions about what happened, and did not happen. The important factor was, again, to turn it into a learning curve for better ways of conducting the process in future, rather than making it a hanging offence!

Despite all, just before their departure to Israel, Geoffrey sent a letter on June 20 to everyone who had been involved in any way in the previous 15 months. They were given updates on the latest situation in the following letter:

TO ALL ENCOURAGERS OF THE JULY FOOTBALL/EDUCATION PROJECT IN IBILLIN

I want you to know that we are now all set to fulfil the project in Israel in July. We have spent the last 12 months planning the project. On July 27 a team of ten men and women will gather in Ibillin, situated roughly between Haifa and Nazareth. We expect about 150 Jewish and Arab children with their leaders, and apprentice football coaches from the area, to join us in what will be a rock in the wilderness and sands of suffering and fear. The task is to bring the children together and to learn, through sport and talk, how to deal with mistrust, and so bring a new dimension to the thinking in Israel.

Our team of ten consists of a superb group of six newly qualified football coaches from the University of Brighton, led by their senior lecturer, Gary Stidder, and our Researcher named Patrick Johnson. Steven Fine, the Executive Director of Maimonides, will be our liaison man with the Jewish community and I will complete the team.

We will be there for a week. In that time they will have coaching in the morning, with the educational and social activities programme in the afternoon. The youngsters will be divided into three age groups from nine to fourteen, and be further divided into teams of mixed race. They will learn to play together as a team in the morning, and in the afternoon they will share together the kind of society/team they want for their future. The week will conclude with a tournament, with mixed teams playing for the cups and medals. Each participant will receive a memento. The British Ambassador has been invited to present the trophies. Olympic Aid and other bodies have been invited to the tournament, and we intend that there will be coverage from the local media and beyond.

You are part of a massive back-up team. You have raised money from the Flora London Marathon. Many of you have provided individual donations. Others have provided ideas, and helped to create a wonderful network of expertise and resource. The British Embassy in Tel Aviv and the British Council have added their insights and encouragement. Throughout the year, the Working Group has steadily moved ahead, as though in a four lap race; gathering support, gathering money, gathering the team and now the last lap of the event. Yet this is but the first round. There is the next round in 2002, and so on thereafter.

We hope you feel encouraged by what has been achieved. Think of us while we are there. And think of us next year. And beyond. On behalf of many, I send you the very warmest appreciation and good wishes.

Shalom, Salaam and God bless you.

The First World Sports Peace Project in Ibillin,
Daily Record, 25 July–3 August 2001

The outline perceptions of daily events were recorded by Geoffrey in a diary format, and presented to the Working Group after the project had concluded. The following items included a number of points raised during, and after, the project.

WEDNESDAY, JULY 25
Patrick Johnson and Steven Fine went as advance party to ensure that everything was in place for the project, and so that the local research by Patrick could begin.

FRIDAY, JULY 27
The bulk of the UK leaders and coaching team travelled from London Heathrow, where the energy was contagious amongst the team. The senior student coach, Helen Goodacre, had brought some 90 extra footballs which somehow were distributed in the suitcases of the coaches! At Tel Aviv we were enthusiastically welcomed by Sohil Haj for the first project, after planning which had gone on for over a year. The representative of Olympic Aid was also there, but surprisingly had not, as suggested, made contact beforehand with Sohil Haj. That seemed odd at the time, but nothing was said as everyone was caught up with the enthusiasm of the moment. The group travelled safely, and in comfort, by minibus to Ibillin. After settling into the local student guest house, they attended a welcome reception at the home of Sohil Haj and met the Ibillin leaders and their team of associates who were also to help greatly throughout the week. It was an exciting start to the project.

SATURDAY, JULY 28
After an excellent Arab breakfast, the team was given a reception at the offices of Ibillin Council by the Mayor of Ibillin, Mr Atif Haj. He and his deputies were most gracious and warm in their welcome. He outlined the problems in the area between Arabs and Jews, and referred to the lack of equality between the two sets of citizens in terms of resources, infrastructure and buildings. At this point it was regrettable that there was not to be an input from Misgav, as it would have avoided any possible perception that

the team had only been given one side of the picture. However, it was an educated group, who were capable of assessing information, and making their own conclusions. Nonetheless one group member was heard to murmur: "No taxation without representation".

While the team went to view the pitch, and the resources there, three others went in two vehicles to Nazareth where Jane Shurrush had assembled all the equipment from England. It had finally all arrived! They then hastened in separate vehicles to Akko (Acre) where everyone was entertained to lunch by Elias Haj, a local Ibillin businessman. He was most generous throughout the week, despite the hospitalisation of his wife. The loan of his car for the week saved the project a serious sum of money. In the evening, the equipment was sorted, and the local petrol station saw to the inflation of some 150 footballs without charge! The team was given a rich taste of local enthusiasm and assistance for the project at the grass roots throughout the day. The evening closed with a full debriefing by Geoffrey, and a full briefing by Gary. The discussion was open, fluent, positive and mature.

SUNDAY, JULY 29

More than 80 children had already assembled, in a variety of kits and clothing, before the coaching team had even arrived! And this was the smallest attendance of the week. Disappointingly, however, there were no girls! There were shrugs and smiles, but no delivery. As the rest were playing, Geoffrey spoke casually through the morning with the local male coach of the girls, whom he knew from previous visits over the years. The next day a small contingent arrived in a single car-load, and the girls were extremely able! The next day, a second car-load arrived! Nothing was said, nor was it necessary. There was an energy and enthusiasm in the air. Eventually this involvement of the girls became quite accepted by the whole project, and it was one that was part of the moving of barriers, which had its beginning, and could be developed in future years. It was mischievously gratifying that a girl was in the team which won the trophy for the older group!

The coaches worked with energy and smiles, which were contagious. It was clear from the outset that this was to be a pleasurable experience, as well as a development of their skills.

Youngsters were divided into small groups and coaching began as they perfected their skills of ball control, passing, shooting, tactical awareness, team work, attack, defence and goal-keeping. It was essential to keep the coaches well supplied with liquid, and to give the children regular breaks, because the temperature was around 90 degrees fahrenheit. Nonetheless, at the end of the first morning, many were still in the open, playing football with zest! The constant supplies of drinking water were also used for dousing the heads of the coaches; soon the bright colour of their distinguishing red caps was streaming into their white project shirts, as the dye surrendered to the prevailing conditions. The caps were soon changed to semi sombreros, bought from a stall, and they looked a strange and unlikely bunch of football coaches, until they got on to the pitch.

Gary Stidder and the staff at the University of Brighton had selected their team well. The leadership of Helen Goodacre had a contagious warmth, ably supported by the planning skills of Eamon Brennan, and the total commitment and reliability of the other coaches, Emma Day, Russell LeFoevre, Charlotte Mills, and Craig Northedge. At the close of the first morning, every player was given a T-shirt with the project logo on the front, plus a pair of shorts. The following day, nearly 100 youngsters appeared in white WSPP shirts and black shorts so that everyone had a common identity.

The project had become a catalyst. The owner of the student guest-house, Mr Khoury, was a highly placed Arab official in the government and responsible for Arab culture. He was expanding on his dream for an Arabi games, similar to the Maccabbi games. This was encouraged as a positive and creative move, despite the obstacles that would surely lie ahead. The notion of how to give a dream the practical support, so that it became a "Dream on Legs", became a live issue, and the term itself that summer became a familiar one.

The team was also on a swift learning curve. The coaches were learning to deal with a different culture, and with the language problem. Steven was repeatedly reassuring the group that the people at Misgav felt badly about their withdrawal, and gave their reasons for it. This was in contrast to the fact that they had been involved in confirming the decision making for two months at the highest level. It was essential to the process that the team acknowledged that something had happened beyond their knowledge and control; that Misgav had not delivered for different reasons, and projects could only learn from this if whatever truth there was became acknowledged as part of the process. Clearly this was a very difficult situation for Steven who had been the liaison man with Misgav. One car load of children from Misgav would have been a positive gesture, as it was with the Arab girls who arrived in two car loads on the second day. Not even one of their assistant coaches arrived. There had to be other reasons which were not available to us. To work in areas of the Middle East means one has to learn to live with the unknown. However, while it created a negative track record for Misgav, there were other Jewish communities in the region of Ibillin who could be contacted in the next 12 months and hopefully they could be included in the future. Fortunately, this matter was happily resolved by the next year and the difficulties were never raised after the conclusion of the project in August. Misgav eventually became key players in the following years of the project.

The late Sunday afternoon gave the opportunity to go to a beach near Haifa, which was a necessary refreshing experience. Dinner in the evening was as guests of the Mayor of Ibillin in a restaurant. Already the Director of Sport for Ibillin, Auni Edris, was talking about how to improve on arrangements for next year! The coaches were enthusing already about how to raise the funds by running in the Flora London Marathon. Happiness became a theme of the week. Late night discussions between Gary and Geoffrey celebrated the positive attitude to the project and the overwhelming nature of the local support and hospitality. The first working day of the project had been full, rich and successful.

MONDAY, JULY 30
The children, looking delighted, were there before the arrival of the coaches at 8 a.m. They were dressed in the shirts and shorts of the project, and looked remarkably different to the first day when they arrived in a variety of attire. None of the coaches could tell the difference between the Christians and the Moslems so that was one barrier broken down. There was also an increase in the number of the children, including the group of girls. At first, they trained apart from the boys, but it was a tonic to see another barrier broken down. However, when they mixed, there was the

sight of one youngster with long flowing hair in particular, playing like a maestro, with a shot that went like a rocket: it was one of the girls! So much for girls not playing football!

The coaching went with energy and enthusiasm all round. The Director of Sport, Auni Edris was already on top of things, and proactive in making suggestions for next year – and it was only Day Two. Patrick Johnson had discussions with Geoffrey, and explored the idea of being financed next year to do more research. He approved and supported Patrick's idea of further research, but pointed out that, as yet, there were no such funds in the project.

The evening was spent quietly at the guest-house, and the team brought in take-aways from the excellent local enterprise, named 'Fast Food'. It was intended that the team, at their own request, would relax that evening instead of being entertained. Unsurprisingly, difficulties, which would emerge from time to time through the day, could be aired during the late evening conversations in the courtyard of the guest-house.

TUESDAY, JULY 31

The atmosphere in the breakfast room seemed friendly and warm, and the guest-house organiser, Raffiq, brought in a birthday cake for Helen Goodacre, as it was her birthday. It was a delightful start to the day. Meantime, the coaching was proceeding with enthusiasm, and people were coming to the stadium to see the project. The coaches had a high level of commitment and spirit, so that there was a feeling of joy throughout the football pitch. Children of all ages were finding their way into teams, and thinking ahead to the next day when the tournament would begin its early stages.

The afternoon was spent with two separate groups. One went to the swimming pool in Misgav, and the other went to the Kibbutz in Tuval. There they were met by an expatriate Englishman named Neil Harris who gave an excellent introduction to the five visitors. Having met him before, and having a good rapport with him, Geoffrey was able to ask about the issue of Misgav. Neil was not surprised, and said: "Put it down to politics". Geoffrey had to leave and went to meet the other group at the Misgav pool, and found things were still in the air. Patrick informed him that someone in the office would like him to go

41

there again for discussions the next day. Geoffrey said that he would gladly see them but because the Misgav office had already closed for the day, and because of the hectic time-table, the meeting would need to be in Ibillin. Nothing more was heard on the matter. It was an example of something that became quite common: that messages would be passed on via a 'go-between' third person, rather than direct contact which was clearly more difficult. That third person frequently seemed to find it difficult to indicate to the first person that they could speak directly, and it was not necessary to go via a 'go-between' third party. It was all part of the learning curve for the British group as well as anyone else.

WEDNESDAY, AUGUST 1

The atmosphere in the breakfast room was again joyful, with the team repeatedly focusing on the pleasures of the previous day, and the needs of the day. The morning was full of activity and pleasure, with the quarter-finals being played, and Eamon in particular having worked out the complications of how the entire group of children could be occupied for the Tournament on the Thursday. On Wednesday, Gary left for England, leaving behind a highly successful operation, with the rest of the coaches highly motivated, and on top of things. That afternoon the coaches went on a kayaking expedition, while Geoffrey reckoned to visit the Social Education section, only to find it was not being held that day, as they had all planned to go kayaking. Unfortunately he never visited a Social Education programme at all, but asked Sohil to give him a breakdown and a report once it was over. It did not appear to have been the success that had been hoped. Wednesday evening was spent at the home of Auni Edris, and it was another wonderful evening with a lovely family.

THURSDAY, AUGUST 2: THE TOURNAMENT AND PRIZE-GIVING

The British Ambassador, His Excellency Francis Cornish, arrived and made himself at ease as Geoffrey introduced him to Helen Goodacre who, in turn, introduced him to the team, and the helpers from Ibillin. Jane Shurrush and Caron Sethill were there from the British Council, and the Mayor of Ibillin, Atif Haj, present with some of his deputies. Sohil acted as interpreter and it was an amazingly energised morning. The games took place, as informal discussions were being held about the project and the overall situation. The Ambassador presented the prizes and gave a speech, as did the Mayor and Geoffrey. Then everyone was presented with gifts, plaques, and statuettes from the community to remember the occasion. The Ambassador's final words to Geoffrey were along the lines of: "What you are doing is so important. It doesn't only help the people, but you help us in our work too. You must do this again". It was a very moving statement and Geoffrey replied, saying that the UK team planned to come again, and he would be kept updated. The Ambassador also spoke with the rest of the team in a free and relaxed way before returning to Tel Aviv. It had been a momentous and historic morning. The project had been successful and there had been a remarkable atmosphere in the community, which had been enhanced by the high profile visit of the Ambassador. The local media conducted interviews, which helped reinforce the status of the project. Moreover, it also indicated that the project was taken seriously in official quarters, Arab, Jewish and English.

The coaches were clear that this had been a wonderful and worthwhile experience. They could have stayed in England and earned money doing vacation jobs but, instead, came to Israel against such a dangerous backcloth and worked for nothing in the height of summer. Yet they were not only enriched themselves, and wished to return, but saw the project as one which they would commend to their fellow students for next year.

The male members of the group had decided to leave that afternoon for Jerusalem for sight-seeing. It had been arranged for them to stay with Geoffrey's contacts in a guest-house in Abu Gosh, ten miles from Jerusalem, and then to be taken to the airport the following day. Geoffrey returned to England on the Thursday afternoon, having arranged for the women in the team to be driven to Akko on the Friday, in a car chauffeured by their barrister host, Raffiq Khoury, for a morning by the Mediterranean Sea. In the afternoon they were taken directly to the airport by the family of Sohil Haj, and returned home.

Geoffrey phoned the Abu Gosh guest-house from Sussex on the Friday morning, and again lunchtime, before the men left Jerusalem, to ensure that they too were well cared for. They were in good hands. He was thankful that things had gone so well, and that the team had remained focused on the primary task of

Conflict Resolution, and had not been deflected from that objective by other matters. They returned triumphant on August 3. Despite the absence of the Jews, and the small number of girls, it had succeeded because it had happened.

FRIDAY, AUGUST 3
Most of the day was a follow up to the very positive contact earlier that morning with the Vice-Chancellor of the University of Brighton, Sir David Watson. When Geoffrey thanked him for his students, and the work they had done, he in turn was both delighted and relieved, and asked for a report which he could present to the Board of Governors. Geoffrey sent copies of Sir David's letter of reply to him, to the families of the coaches, and to the coaches themselves. Letters of thanks were also sent to all who had helped directly in Ibillin, as well as the British Council and the British Embassy. In addition he contacted Johann Olav Koss of Olympic Aid, and initiated an exchange of information about their policy regarding sending a Jew or an Arab to a project which involved both communities.

Conclusions

The project was a success, despite the non-arrival of the Jewish children, and should be continued; there had been a further excellent improvement and development of the existing track record with the town of Ibillin which went back to 1993. The morning of the final tournament was memorable as the British Ambassador presented the trophies and medals, with his attendance giving a significant profile to the project and for its future. Members of the British Council were also present and found, to their great pleasure, that the project was sound, far reaching, had great promise, and worthy of their support in the future. Equally the Mayor of Ibillin and his deputies were present and fulsome in their praise and support, because it had created a stimulus in the neighbourhood and beyond. It was sad that the people who were sorely missed were the Jewish children, but hopefully they would be able to attend another year.

In contemplating the future, it was possible to consider that the project could link initiatives with the British Council's "Dreams

44

and Teams" enterprise and that the Ibillin event could be combined with them in 2002. Moreover, Ibillin could make contact with other Jewish groups within their own political region to encourage their participation next year. In the UK, the project for 2002 could be simplified by Geoffrey and David having responsibility for the overall scheme, and liaising directly with the University of Brighton and the British Embassy, as well as the local authorities in Israel. After the success of the initial project, it was good to feel the increase in interest in Israel, especially of Misgav and the British Council. For the next summer project, the Chelsea School of Physical Education of Brighton University would be encouraged to find another team of coaches for the last week of August 2002. Moreover, the School would liaise with the Flora London Marathon, so that students could raise the funds for the WSPP by sponsorship of their participation in the event.

It was also noted that there needed to be greater care in relation to future association with individuals and outside bodies. Implied in this was the sense that any involvement with others called for those with experience, expertise and impartiality. This had not always been discerned, and a more careful policy of co-operation and involvement needed to be developed. It was essential to notice the significant and crucial difference between the many people and organisations who professed enthusiasm, and those who actually delivered on their interest. It meant that the project had to be able to hurdle the setbacks and non-delivery of promises with professional equanimity, and not to take offence when disappointed.

For the project it was a rich learning curve, and plans were already in hand for another initiative the next year, which would benefit from the lessons of the previous year. The leaders were a small part of a great team of people, who encouraged the project through their support, their energy, their money and their prayers. All were part of peace making. After all, they had not been far from the place where a certain person gave the Sermon on the Mount! There the group saw inscribed, the words in St Matthew's gospel: 'Blessed are the peacemakers for they shall be called the sons of God'. Indeed.

A significant outcome was the effect on the coaches from the University of Brighton. Despite the conditions and the difficulties, there had been an ongoing flow of enthusiasm throughout the project. This continued afterwards when there was a get-together in Eastbourne of a number of the team. It had become apparent that the experience had stood them in good stead, not only personally, but professionally. Indeed, one of the students had left college and, on the basis of her CV which included her work in the project, she was successful in her job application. She herself put it down to her participation in Israel, and the impression this had made on those who scrutinised her application, and who interviewed her.

It was hoped that the input of the University of Brighton would be as excellent in the future as at the time. There needed to be clear divisions of responsibility in the organisation of future projects, and mutual understanding about the relationships with other organisations that would come on board. The WSPP needed to have the ultimate responsibility for decisions about policy, participation and finance, until it could find larger, separate organisations who could be trusted to take responsibility for its future. This last point was prophetic in view of developments post-Galilee 2003. With hindsight, one can see that the project had already progressed well and had made the essential relationships that would take the vision of Geoffrey and David further in the country and beyond. Both the University of Brighton and the British Council had the staff to do the administration, and the skilled personnel to organise, manage, develop and conduct the project in future years.

The plans for a larger, second project in the summer of 2002 were being made within a few weeks. That event was to include the community of Misgav, and that of Tivon, and there would be over 150 children participating.

3

Developments from September 2001 to the Second Project, 2002

The second project in the summer of 2002 was to become larger in every way than that of the previous year. It was to involve more youngsters from more communities, with a larger team from the UK, greater expense, and even more learning curves. Despite a background of ongoing violence in other parts of the country, the project gathered pace and influence, and acted as a working model for co-existence for those who wished to see with their eyes and hear with their ears. Before this could be put into effect there were significant developments to be undertaken.

To prepare for the second project, it was clear that there was an even greater energy and commitment ready to plan ahead for it, with a firm emphasis on engaging the participation of the Jews and a larger contingent of girls. In addition, because of the short-comings of the Social Education sector, there was still significant progress to be made in the development of that part of the oper-ation. Despite the fact that there were people in the Working Group who had experience of conflict work, those skills were not sufficiently well honed and harnessed to bring about any sense of achievement, apart from the children having met together, and a local organisational base being set in place. The strength of the project could be seen in its self-awareness when it acknowledged its lack of experience or expertise and needed to find extra resources.

Importantly, before the future planning could be begun in September 2001 onwards, there were pleasurable matters of appreciation and courtesy to be addressed. One of the factors that had enabled the group to build such a successful network was the relationships that had been created. These courtesies were not difficult, although time consuming, because there was a genuine appreciation of those in the background who had given so much help, as distinct from the tasks of those directly involved. This support had given special warmth to the interactions over the previous 15 months, and was to be a creative factor over the three and a half years of the project.

It was also essential to create and sustain a policy of appreciation in other directions. Apart from letters to the coaches and their leaders which could go into their CVs for future reference, it was important to write to their families and to tell them of the appreciation of the Co-Founders. All had allowed their loved ones to go to a place that was not the safest in the world and they kept their anxieties to themselves. Then there were letters to the suppliers of equipment and assistance, many unseen and out of the public eye in the UK and Israel.

The letter of appreciation to the Vice-Chancellor of the University of Brighton, Sir David Watson, was most warmly received, which he then presented to the Board of Governors. Finally, there were letters of celebration to people of goodwill such as Nelson Mandela and Desmond Tutu, from whom there were gracious responses and messages of warmth. Nelson Mandela had been invited to become the patron of the project, and the reluctance in his regretful non-acceptance was almost tangible.

First steps for the Second Project, 2002

September 2001 soon arrived and, again, it was down to business, with a measure of confidence from what had been achieved, and the mistakes, from which there could be rich learning for the future. There was also a background of dismay because of the attacks on the United States by Al Qaeda. Yet because Geoffrey had been in New York City on September 11, he was able that week to meet with staff of another organisation, Seeds of Peace

(SoP), and explore future collaboration. SoP had a project for conflict resolution which took Arab and Jewish youngsters from Israel to a summer camp venue in the USA. This was a different concept to the WSPP which worked in the local area, rather than removing them from their own region. Having made the connection, the link was established with their office in Jerusalem and their programme director, Ned Lazarus. The network was on the increase still.

The reports of the project were distributed to the Working Group for their meeting on September 25. It was acknowledged that there was disappointment at the withdrawal of the Jews from Misgav, but that there would naturally be a great deal to learn from what was the first such project. However, it was to be celebrated that the project had taken place and had received such enthusiastic responses from the community, constructive support from the British Embassy, and the early, tentative involvement of the British Council.

It was simple to agree to offer a similar project to Ibillin, and to seek to liaise with the Embassy and the British Council, for 2002. Moreover, it was seen as essential that the local community ensured the participation of Jewish and Arab children in both football and Social Education. It was also agreed that the University of Brighton would again supply the coaching team, and funds would be raised by their team of runners at the Flora London Marathon. It was anticipated that Geoffrey would make a visit to Ibillin in November to continue the close contact with the local organisers there.

There was some discussion about the title of the organisation, ranging from the original 'Sussex Sports for Peace', 'World Sports Peace Project' to 'Sport for World Peace'. Subsequently the title agreed on was 'World Sports Peace Project' because it represented the original vision of Geoffrey and David that the project could extend on a global scale.

Geoffrey's next visit to Israel and the West Bank in November resulted in further significant developments and one huge step forward. There were four events that stood out in particular for their massive significance.

49

The preparatory visit to Israel, November 2001 and developments with the British Council

The first significant event was a meeting on November 7, with the British Council in Tel Aviv which included the Director, David Elliott, Caron Sethill from the West Jerusalem office, and Jane Shurrush of the Nazareth office who had given assistance in obtaining the equipment from Israeli customs in July. Geoffrey had maintained friendly relations with them after the project so they knew of his visit to prepare for the summer of 2002. They invited him to meet with them and the meeting, which was friendly and relaxed, led to their structured involvement in the future. Clearly they had been impressed with what World Sports Peace Project had accomplished in a relatively short space of time. From their almost 'observer' position in July, they were wishing to find out more about the project in order to decide whether or not to become more involved and proactively supportive.

The British Council had a proven track record in promoting many cultural activities and exchanges, but community sport at this level had not been their prime consideration. Probably the approach of WSPP appeared all very unusual; there had been no application forms in a quest for funding or resources – purely a polite indication of their intentions by way of information and as a matter of courtesy. Indeed the project not only had a background of community work since 1993, but WSPP had mounted the project well before the British Council came on the scene earlier that summer. It was probably all quite curious because it had not passed through the normal, predictable channels. Nonetheless, the project must have 'passed muster' with this official body, because of the quality and successful outcome of the summer event, which had unfolded before their eyes. Under the leadership of the director, David Elliott, they enquired about the project, its background, formation and intentions for the future. The fact that it was being conducted on an unpaid basis by people who had respected backgrounds in other spheres and had come into being in only eighteen months seemed to have a fascination for those who were impressed by the outcome they had witnessed. There appeared to be neither ulterior motives, guile, nor hidden agendas on the part of WSPP, and the meeting was very cordial, in spite of the unorthodox nature of the operation which seemed to have caused some surprise.

With hindsight, that unorthodoxy had probably enabled the project to get off the ground because the working group consisted of individuals who were keen and committed to it. The working culture of the WSPP had been one of pragmatic excellence. They had not had to seek approval from other agencies, but rather colleagueship. There had been no applications to any organisations for permission, but invitations were given to others to become involved. It is possible that, in future years, the project would be more complicated to bring to pass. Most importantly however, the project had begun at the grassroots, with an already established youth organisation in a municipality. The football/conflict prevention development was simply an extension of something quite small and local in Ibillin. Only later did it expand very swiftly to the extent that it became international and cross-cultural. The fact that organisations like the British Council wished to come on board meant that they brought with them different, more orthodox and formal working cultures of control, administration and accountability. They were different to the more relaxed and inter-personal dynamics of the highly motivated group of independent experts who had started the project in 2000.

The Council wished to understand the responsibility of the key players in the local planning teams in and around Ibillin, with emphases on professional attitudes and accountability. It was warming to notice their immediate task-centredness on a range of issues, including providing assistance for the participation of Jewish children. It appeared to be well understood that this was crucial to Geoffrey and David's original vision of Arab–Jewish participation. It was essential to keep one's eyes on the short-term aim of bringing children together from separate communities, and the long-term aim of developing it in such a way that it would be continued locally after the UK initiative by the WSPP had been entrusted to others. Although it could not have been predicted, less than two years later the British Council was so entrusted by the WSPP.

What was problematic was the fact that the Second Intifada had broken out since the tournament in the Summer. Already there was bloodshed and destruction further in the south so that the Israeli Defence Force was mobilised and hostilities were in abundance. There was a massive breakdown in relationships between the Jews and Arabs. The election of Prime Minister Sharon was perceived by some to provoke violence by both sides and each consistently blamed the other and justified their own position. In the Galilee area there was an undercurrent of anxiety about how things might develop and about inter-community relations. This was not an easy backcloth to plan for future Jewish–Arab connections. It was important not to lose the momentum of the project and the favourable publicity which had been attracted, partly because of the high profile visit of the British Ambassador and the local enthusiasm which had been generated. Thus the creation and support of the local planning group was essential for the future. At a time when there was an increasing sense of fear and distrust, there was a positive symbol of harmony and hope in their midst which was clearly a positive alternative for good.

Formal recognition and honouring of the project in Ibillin

The second event took place in the council offices of Ibillin on November 10 when the Mayor and Council made Geoffrey an Honorary Citizen of the town. This was a great honour for Geoffrey, as a Christian, to receive such a tribute from a Moslem Mayor and council. This was in recognition of the quality of the input over the years, all of which had been voluntarily provided for the benefit of a whole generation of young people from the town. The award had come from both Moslem and Christian people and in retrospect, although it was not noticed at the time, no official religious person from either community had taken any initiative or become involved in any interaction; it was the civic administration that took the lead and set the seal on this phase of the development.

Strategies for turning blame into learning curves

The third event took place after the award ceremony, with a meeting with the core planning team in Ibillin, where a number of matters were discussed. Principally the issue of Misgav was raised and their future participation. Unfortunately they were still involved in blaming others for their late withdrawal from the project in July. It seemed essential to be able to move on and not to be deterred by such attitudes, so that, if they could come in with a fresh beginning and management, the way ahead for joint working was possible.

The model for future co-operation was thereby established, in order that future projects could not be sabotaged by issues of blame. Having settled that issue it was possible, quite swiftly, to outline the process of planning for the next project which would be held from 22–29 August 2002. Moreover, it was agreed that the local planning team in Israel would meet every two or three weeks with Jane Shurrush of the British Council to ensure that progress was in good order. This turned out to be an increasingly complex undertaking, but it was a very new venture and it was inevitable that it would not be a simple undertaking. Nonetheless it was essential to expand the notion of regular and consistent co-operation between the communities. Even at that very early stage, it was necessary to construct and strengthen the bridges so that by the time the project reached its third year in 2003, the structures would be recognisable as a working scheme.

It was essential to keep in mind that the project was voluntary and the only authority was built on the teamwork of colleague-ship, goodwill and focus on the primary task which was bigger than any member of the group. That bottom-up *esprit de corps* could not be built on authority and control, but on consensus and respect.

West Bank beginnings in Bethlehem

The fourth event took place on the night after returning from Jerusalem and moving on to Bethlehem on Sunday, November 11. Geoffrey had dinner with a Palestinian couple from the Greek Orthodox Community, Faiz and Norma Hanona, with whom he had worked for a number of years. Hence there was a tremendous bridge of trust and confidence that had been constructed and well-maintained over a significant period of time. In talking over the events in Ibillin, Faiz wanted to know why there was not a similar project in Bethlehem. "Why don't you come here?" he simply asked. Geoffrey agreed that it would be a good idea, but said that there were no football pitches in the area. "We have two", Faiz replied. Very quickly it was agreed that if Faiz could form a committee to take forward the idea, then it could be discussed in detail with them during the next visit in early spring.

Geoffrey was pleased at the swift Palestinian initiative, but could not see how it would be possible to include the Jews immediately, although it could happen eventually as co-existence improved – indeed Faiz was clear that there would be Jews who would already wish to participate. Accordingly the WSPP informed the British Council in Tel Aviv and West Jerusalem who, in turn, informed them that the British Council offices in East Jerusalem covered affairs in the West Bank and not in Israel. Contact with the office in East Jerusalem was also speedily established and so the project would speedily move beyond Israel. Similar initiatives involved contact with the Consulate General in East Jerusalem, which had responsibility for the West Bank, rather than the British Embassy in Tel Aviv which had responsibility in Israel. The vision was developing, but it was not realised how swiftly the notion would take off by the following March, despite the violence that was already taking place elsewhere.

Strengthening the organisational bases

The Working Group met in London on November 26 to confirm, among other things, the findings of the visit and to plan further for the improvements of the August project. In particular this meant closer liaison with the British Council and the Arab–Jewish community in Ibillin and its region. It was felt that the development in the West Bank, while welcome, could be discussed with them during the next visit in March, but was unlikely to be possible for a number of years. This turned out to be very mistaken!

Meanwhile, good communication had been established between Geoffrey, the British Council and Ibillin and it seemed that the aims were compatible and the work well understood. However, there would always be hitches in the undertaking of responsibilities of such a young and growing enterprise, and such was the case over the coming months. Nonetheless, the permanent attitude was to endeavour to be undeterred by such hitches, by having a positive mental attitude throughout. Thus the project overcame obstacles and proceeded on its journey.

Just before Christmas, Patrick Johnson sent his successful MA thesis which was very informative and useful. Inevitably there were a few different perceptions, but what was very enlightening was the outcome of his meetings in the summer with people in Misgav. It became clear that a number of different people had been involved at different stages, and their own internal communication systems were not sufficiently well organised for the agreements made by some to be carried forward by the next layer of leadership. The tendency to blame others was unfortunate, but needed not to be an obstacle for future work together.

By January 2002 there was an ever-growing demand for time to attend to the increasing load of administration for the project in the summer. Geoffrey was assigned to carry this responsibility and it became a matter of necessity for him to deal with issues on a daily basis, which became virtually a full-time task. On 8 January there was another meeting of the Working Group, this time at the University of Brighton in Eastbourne. David Bedford came to brief those who would run the Marathon in April, thereby raising the funds for the next project in August.

The Working Group had been reduced to five in number, namely Geoffrey and David, John Sugden and Gary Stidder from the Chelsea School of Education of the University of Brighton and Laurie Robinson, the management consultant. There was also a large resource group in the background, from whom to draw as the need arose. Circulation of the notes of each meeting was made to a range of people who were in that resource group, as well as the planning team in Israel at the British Council and Ibillin.

The meeting had its usual task-centred style, focusing on the visit to Ibillin over the first weekend in March, followed by arrangements within the University for the team of Marathon runners in April, and the football coaches in August. The issues were quite simple for the WSPP had constructed its own way of working which was both efficient and effective.

The March visit would involve Geoffrey, together with John Sugden and Gary Stidder from the University. They would meet the potential Jewish and Arab groups in Ibillin and discuss details of organisation at meetings organised by the British Council in Nazareth. This would be followed by exploring resources in Jerusalem and Bethlehem for possible visits after the summer project, and discussions for eventual projects in the West Bank.

The university arrangements for both tasks were already in place and, in particular, the university planned to include the Social Education aspect of the project within the overall coaching of the youngsters. This had not been successful in 2001, and a fresh strategy was to be used in 2002. It was also decided that John and Gary would lead a team of eight coaches from the Chelsea School of Physical Education from August 22–29.

There was a third essential matter which was raised. Geoffrey asked the question of whether or not he would need to be present at the project itself in the summer, because the time had to come when he was no longer essential to the project. This was not pursued but left with the assumption that he would attend. These were still early days and Geoffrey had been the instigator of a wide range of relationships with other organisations in the area, notably: World Vision, Christian Aid, New Israel Fund, and Seeds of Peace. It was considered not the time to leave the project, but Geoffrey had needed it to be flagged for action in the fore-seeable future.

At the end of the Working Group meeting, the Marathon runners were to be assembled to receive briefings by Geoffrey and David. John anticipated that they would raise £10,000 for the costs of the project. That briefing meeting took place with great enthusiasm and energy and there was the adrenalin of expecta-tion in the air. Geoffrey and John had additionally prepared separate papers for publicity and it was agreed that Laurie could use them and produce an acceptable document as promotional material for distribution in the UK and Israel. It had been a creative start to the year.

By January 17, there had been a meeting in Ibillin with repre-sentatives from Tivon and Misgav, joining in an agreement to be involved in a project in the summer. It was noticeable that Misgav had shown a keenness to be included this year, as though they had been surprised that the project in 2001 could proceed success-fully without them. The non-aggressive reaction to their behaviour in that year had clearly enabled the project to move on without a residue of ill-will. Sohil also confirmed that the three mayors of the town would meet with the English representatives on March 3, together with Jane Shurrush of the British Council in Nazareth. In support of the logistical arrangements for February and March, the community with the guest-house in Abu Gosh confirmed that they would provide accommodation and transportation during the March visit.

In the same week, on January 19, the Ibillin Director of Sport, Auni Edris, made contact to confirm the details of the football side of the project. Sohil Haj, who had been the leading figure for a number of years in the relations with Ibillin, was focused on the social education factor. Auni was a man who had impressive experience of sport, and football in particular. Both were experts in their own fields, but not in each other's, and it was easier to interact with them separately, in relation to their expertise. This was productive, as long as the issues did not overlap. They had their own ways of working and their own value systems, which led to great strengths, but also natural differences. Clearly, however, a great deal was coming into being in Ibillin.

On February 20, Geoffrey wrote to the colleagues in the UK and Israel, covering the progress so far. He concluded:

Dear Friends,
There is a murmur within me; we are embarked on a great enterprise which will have far-reaching effects on the generations to come, after we are all gone. We shall accomplish it, be sure, as part of the contribution of our generation. We are only small cogs in the wheel of something bigger than ourselves, whatever name we give to the Ground of our Being, 'Our calling to fulfil, To serve the present age'.

By February 25, Jane Shurrush wrote to indicate that progress was well under way and it was possible to consider including some of the young people of the area taking responsibility for some of the Social Education. That evening, Geoffrey, still three days before departure, made contact with the wider planning teams and raised 14 specific points concerning the fine detail of the project, which needed to be discussed at the joint meeting the following week. Within 48 hours, Auni Edris had responded, also in detail. The partnership was working even more efficiently.

The clouds, the rainbow and the commitment, March 2002

Despite the worsening situation of violence throughout Israel and the West Bank between Arab and Jew, everyone was focused on the primary task of Conflict Resolution and football. Geoffrey, John and Gary left early the following morning for Jerusalem. True to their word, the sisters at Abu Gosh had sent their driver to collect them at Ben-Gurion airport and they checked into their homely guesthouse. They confirmed that it would be possible for the group to stay there after Ibillin in August and to use it as a base for seeing the Old City before returning to the UK.

The following morning, March 1, there were stories of increased military activity and shootings at night. Nonetheless the three leaders went into Jerusalem for a meeting with Caron Sethill at the American Colony Hotel. It was a very task-centred meeting of minds. There was a change from the observational, interest stance of last year, to one of direct involvement and the need for clear exchanges of information regarding the details of the operation between all the partners. Details about the Social Education programme were taken up, and the new stance on security in relation to the worsening situation was also high on the list. Moreover, there needed to be clear understanding between the partners about what each expected, and what each could, and could not, provide.

There were two more meetings that morning, both of which were profitable in ensuring the continuing networking and good-will between WSPP and other international Non-Governmental Organisations (NGOs). The first was at the office of World Vision and a meeting with the Director, Dan Simmons, with whom Geoffrey had already been in contact. World Vision had worked in Ibillin for many years and Geoffrey had had associations with them since 1995. So again, there was a well constructed bridge of trust and confidence, over which they, mutually, could cross. Dan was very supportive of the project and was willing to assist, particularly with any local arrangements and sensitivities.

Mention has already been made that Geoffrey had met with the organisation, Seeds of Peace, while marooned in New York, on 13 September 2001, two days after the destruction of the World Trade Centre. It had been a constructive meeting between the two heads of organisations which had so much in common in terms of conflict prevention and community relationships. The difference was the WSPP brought Arab and Jewish children together from the local communities within Israel, rather than taking them from the situation and placing the projects in different parts of the USA. Moreover the scale of operation was different, Seeds of Peace being well funded, with permanent staff and offices in Manhattan and elsewhere. In Jerusalem they met with Ned Lazarus, the director in Israel, who was warm and supportive, being willing to visit the project in August.

At the end of an excellent morning's further bridge building, the three were taken to Bethlehem where they had to pass through the checkpoint to enter the town. There was a queue of Palestinians waiting in the line and, as was his way, Geoffrey engaged the Israeli soldiers in conversation as they made their way through. It was simpler to do than if one were an Arab and had to wait and endure the interrogations and humiliations of the search, together with suspicion and mutual dislike.

It was a relief to arrive at the convent of the Franciscan Sisters of Mary – The White Sisters – and to be greeted by a succession of elderly, gentle, smiling ladies, who largely spoke French! Sister Maria spoke fluent English and was a wonderful hostess. The convent was situated at the rear of the Church of the Holy Nativity, and shortly the grounds were to be occupied by Israeli troops as they mounted guard over the church, with Palestinians taking refuge inside. It was also the base of the Holy Family Care Centre, which was a therapeutic unit for victims of the Intifada. Geoffrey had worked there for a number of years, but this time they were the only guests, because the shootings every night made pilgrims a rarity. Worse was soon to come.

An arrangement had been made with Faiz Hanona to meet with his committee to discuss the possibility of conducting a similar project in the Bethlehem area. John Sugden was positive about the idea, but reasonably thought it would not happen for five years or more. The committee arrived very late that night and Faiz had included George Rishmawi, of the Rapprochement Centre and Elias Al-Atrash from the Greek Orthodox Club and Community Centre. It turned into a powerful meeting of minds and hearts as the trio from England sat down and soon were listening to three men who were far more cognisant of the complexities of the situation than they were themselves. They had an expertise and political sophistication which was quite humbling for the visitors. It was clear that they were way ahead of the game and had much to teach the Englishmen. They were far more aware of the need to be involved in the work of Conflict Prevention, even more than Conflict Resolution and so the focus changed. It was soon apparent that the three from the UK were privileged to listen to men who worked daily in a situation of immense social and political extremity, and learned from them.

Before the evening was over, many things had moved on. Instead of 'waiting until they were ready', the WSPP leaders indicated that they would bring their team immediately following the project in Ibillin and, instead of staying in Abu Gosh, they would come to Bethlehem for a three day project before returning home. Geoffrey asked that they should see the sports facilities before they departed and they agreed to meet again the following day. There had been a complete and happy turn around.

The following morning, the leaders from the community of Beit Sahour, a suburb of Bethlehem, showed the visitors the resources which were centred in the Greek Orthodox Club. Faiz, who had initiated the meetings, simply allowed his colleagues to conduct the remainder of the exercise. There were many facilities for the unemployed and the youth. Of fundamental interest was the visit to the almost completed football stadium. The visitors were introduced to Attallah El Hayek, the manager of the stadium, who was vigorous and enthusiastic – another visionary who could see the relevance of the project that was envisaged for August. Although the pitch still needed to be cleared of stones, there were fine resources almost immediately available, especially the buildings and the supportive community. They had a clear mindset of the needs that would be present long after the Jewish problem was settled. Conflict Prevention was at the heart of their work, not least between Christian and Moslem Arabs, and from then on this became the primary focus of the British team. Already in Beit Sahour they had the manpower and ability to harness the resources for the visit in August. If the project leaders could bring the coaches, the local committee would see to the rest of the arrangements in Bethlehem/Beit Sahour.

It was agreed to recommend that the football equipment be entrusted to the British Council in East Jerusalem for collection and use, immediately after the project in Ibillin. Because of the politics, it would be essential to see the project in Beit Sahour as quite separate from the one in Ibillin. Activities in Israel and the West Bank were clearly divided into two separate responsibilities by the authorities. The British Embassy and the British Council in Israel related directly to the Israeli authorities but not in Palestine. So, for events in the West Bank, the connections already separately made by Geoffrey with the East Jerusalem offices of the Consul General and the British Council would be developed immediately on return to the UK. A final meeting to sort out logistics for the project was arranged for that evening.

Ominously, there were other meetings, the most significant being with the Director of Applied Research Institute – Jerusalem, Dr Jad Isaac. He became worried when he knew of their intention to meet that evening before returning to Israel the next day. He gravely advised the team to leave for Jerusalem that very afternoon: "Because the Israelis are going to invade Bethlehem in the next 24 hours. They will be coming with their tanks to shell us and to crush us," he said. The date was 2 March 2002. The team felt they could not leave until they had fulfilled their commitment, despite the seriousness of his words. Jad extracted the promise from Geoffrey that if he phoned the group by mobile phone, then they would leave immediately without delay, because the invasion would have already started.

That evening the new colleagues from Beit Sahour, amidst the sound of gunfire and shelling, took them to the underground cavern restaurant, appropriately named "The Citadel", to discuss more detailed arrangements over a meal and to become closer as a team. There would be another 100 children involved in their project that summer, to add to the 200 separately in Ibillin. In the following years, it could be extended and become of increasing significance. It was dark in the restaurant, but six men were planning something akin to a light in the darkness. During one point in the gunfire, Geoffrey murmured: "We represent a Rainbow in Bethlehem tonight." It was an unforgettable experience – as was the journey back to the convent. The phone did not ring that night, and in the morning they left behind the storm that was about to break. It was 3 March 2002. Three years later Bethlehem was still under occupation and The Separation Wall was being built around the people to enclose them from Jerusalem and much of the West Bank.

The following day, they went by bus to Haifa where they were met by Sohil. The day moved apace, with significant separate phases. First, despite the assurances about attendance, perhaps because it was a working day and volunteers could not be present, the first meeting was held with only Sohil and Auni of Ibillin from the local leadership. Nonetheless it was possible to clarify a number of matters. In particular it was confirmed that a UK team of eight coaches, under the leadership of Geoffrey, John and Gary, would be present at the combined Football/Conflict Prevention project for the mixed communities of Arabs and Jews from August 22–29. It was intended that the first two days would be spent with the local coaching team, in preparation for the work with children from the three communities of Ibillin, Tivon and Misgav. Moreover the UK would provide the equipment of footballs and shirts. The British Ambassador or his deputy would present the prizes at the tournament on the final day.

In turn, for their part, Auni Edris and Sohil Haj planned with their Jewish colleagues to open the project in Ibillin, with its better resources, on the Sunday; visit Tivon and Misgav on the following two days and conclude in Ibillin on the Wednesday and Thursday. Between them, they planned to provide 150 children, aged between 10 and 14, of mixed gender and race. In addition there would be 12 assistant coaches to work with the coaches from the UK. They would also provide the necessary resources and equipment, including first aid and refreshments. The coaches would also receive transportation, a visiting programme and accommodation. A registration list of participating children would be compiled in advance, as well as advertising, promotion and publicity. In addition to the Social Education Programme, there would be a social programme, with special arrangements for the inclusion of disabled children and those with special needs. It all seemed gratifyingly extensive and inclusive. But could it be delivered?

The next meeting, which took place at the Ibillin Council Offices, was a unique and historic occasion, attended by a large number of representatives from the Arab and Jewish communities. The Mayors of Ibillin and Misgav, together with the Ombudsman, representing the Mayor of Tivon, gave speeches of welcome for the initiatives of the World Sports Peace Project, and also recognised the work of the local community leaders who had worked hard to bring about the second project. They promised warmth and hospitality to everyone involved. It was pointed out that they recognised the project as a move towards better relationships which could have positive lasting effect on the people of the country. The Mayor of Misgav particularly expressed his pleasure that what had not been successfully completed last year would now happen in 2002. The vision of 2000 was taking shape before their eyes, less than two years later. In other parts of the land there were tanks in the streets, helicopters in the sky, and death and destruction in abundance. In Ibillin that morning it was not so.

In the afternoon, Geoffrey returned to Jerusalem to follow up the networks already established, while John and Gary visited the sports facilities in the area. It was another fruitful meeting at the British Embassy the following day when Geoffrey again met Mark Kelly in Tel Aviv. There was a sense of moving on, from the small but highly successful beginning the previous year, to something of increasing significance. Apart from the immediate encouragement for the growth of the project, there was the assurance that it was probable that the trophies and medals could be presented by the Deputy British Ambassador, Mr Peter Carter, if the new Ambassador was not in place by August.

To recapitulate, it was important to ensure that the two projects, one in Israel and the other in the West Bank, were kept separate, not least because there were separate diplomatic offices in relation to both the Foreign and Commonwealth Office and for the British Council, as well as for the local planning teams in each area. In relation to the NGOs however, World Vision and Seeds of Peace covered both areas, which made planning that much simpler. As a result, the WSPP related to the British Embassy and the British Council in Tel Aviv for the projects in Israel, while the Consul General and the British Council in East Jerusalem had the interest in the projects in the West Bank. From then on, the Working Group in Britain had separate agendas for the two projects, with different resource groups.

On reporting back to the Working Group on March 14, it was possible to confirm what had been put in the report of the visit and to clarify the moves behind the surprising development in the West Bank. Geoffrey had already communicated the development in the West Bank to the planning team in Ibillin. In relation to the University of Brighton, John and Gary confirmed that both the teams of Marathon runners and football coaches were in place. The issue of research still remained to be organised. The publicity arrangements were going well with a draft brochure produced by Laurie and contact made with a number of media sources in newspapers, radio and television. It was also planned to contact Premiership football clubs for their support. It seemed essential to maintain contact with the organisations and individuals, such as Olympic Aid, which had been helpful in the previous year's project, as well as the resource people involved during the critical early period in the development of the work.

It was agreed that the two projects would run in August and that the coaching team would move from Ibillin to the West Bank and continue with the second project, before leaving for the UK as planned on the Sunday. There was one proviso – that if the security situation made it inadvisable to travel with staff and students, and having taken advice from the Foreign and Commonwealth Office, it might be essential to postpone the visit and to return to the UK directly.

Before the end of the month Geoffrey had written to the team of selected football coaches, and more immediately to the Marathon runners, thanking them for their commitment and wishing them well.

During April there were a number of exchanges of correspondence between Geoffrey and Jane Shurrush of the British Council in Nazareth in order to ensure the smooth preparation of the project. It was not always simple for Jane to sustain communications and verbal agreements between the different communities and herself; local communities had their own ways of conducting business and these were still early days of Anglo–Arab–Jewish collaboration. In England, Geoffrey and the University worked to ensure that there was the maximum communication between themselves and with the British Council. They discovered that the administrative processes were complex, frustrating and time consuming. Issues, particularly matters of finance between the three communities, became difficult to resolve. The British Council had expectations of those with whom they worked in Israel and the separate local systems were regularly different and could sometimes lead to frustrations. It was required that each community should put in writing what they expected to cover in terms of costs and this was to become an elusive item for the British Council.

On April 29, Geoffrey learned some devastating news. Their friend and colleague from Beit Sahour, Attallah El Hayek, who was the manager of the sports stadium, had been shot and killed by the occupying Israeli troops. Apparently he had been sent to fetch the keys to the building by the troops and then, as he was so doing, he was shot dead by a patrol. Geoffrey immediately contacted the Rapprochement Centre in the West Bank to discover more details and to express his shock and sadness, for someone whom they already considered as a friend and colleague in Conflict Prevention. As more communication followed, it became clear that Bethlehem was experiencing a terrifying, destructive Israeli invasion force, hitherto unknown.

On May 13, two weeks later, there was a daunting security update from the Foreign and Commonwealth Office which affected the plans for Bethlehem and the West Bank. It strongly advised against travel to the West Bank. The Working Group was not surprised, but already it put a further cloud on their hopes. The Group agreed that if the project was allowed to take place in the West Bank in August, it should be called the 'Rainbow' Project, as a testimony to their colleague, Attallah El Hayek. Planning continued, despite the knowledge that there was a strong possibility that the project might have to be postponed, but certainly not cancelled.

In the meantime, the Working Group continued with the detailed planning for the Ibillin project. The arrangements were at an advanced stage in the UK and it was agreed that another visit might have to be made to Ibillin in July to ensure that the situation in Ibillin was also well in hand. It was emerging that the Jewish groups in Tivon and Misgav were keen to meet for football, but not for the more important side of the project, whether it was called 'Conflict Prevention' or 'Social Education'. There was the sense that, to date, the British Council and Ibillin were more proactive on that half of the project than the other partners.

Not every lead was productive, however, despite a lot of work being put in. Andy Hansen of the British Council informed the Working Group of a new organisation which might value a connection with the project. This was followed up several times by Geoffrey, but there was no response to the initiatives he made by way of invitation to meetings in London or Sussex. Contact had also been made with one of the helpful Moslem resource persons, who suggested a colleague who might help in the West Bank. This was followed up by Geoffrey, but contact by phone and letter received no response, after early enthusiasm and meetings in the Midlands. It was important to recognise that people and organisations might show genuine early enthusiasm for the project, but not all carried that through with tangible support. Support took a number of forms, from emotional encouragement and advice and the desire for information, to the supply of knowledge, equipment and fund-raising. There was still no 'manual' on how to conduct such a project, but gradually it was writing itself.

More clouds in the lead up to the Second Project

Because of extreme acts of violence by both sides, the security situation in Israel and the West Bank had deteriorated. Geoffrey therefore wrote to the families of the coaches on June 9, to thank them for their support. In addition, he informed them that the project would be monitored by the British Embassy and British Council in relation to the security situation. He also wrote to the teams in Israel and the West Bank, as well as the resource groups in the UK and elsewhere, giving them an update on the two projects as they were perceived by the Working Group. There was optimism about their taking place, but realism about the background situation which could bring about changes, even at the last minute. He wrote:

We are all engaged in a critically important set of projects at such a serious time as this. It will call for the best from each of us. Whatever is the outcome, now and in the future, let it be seen that we have given our finest to the tasks. The events on a daily basis in Israel and Palestine are so distressing that they could be disheartening. Let us keep the vision of two peoples living in harmony, with justice, peace and security for them all. That is what our projects embody.

However, there was further disappointment in the UK.

Having expected £10,000 from the money raised in the Flora London Marathon, Geoffrey had to advise the Working Group on July 9 that only £5,000 had been received. Although John and Gary accepted that their original target of £10,000 had not been reached, they had still expected it to reach £8,000. John said that the Chelsea School of Physical Education of the University of Brighton would provide £1,000 towards the shortfall, but this did not materialise.

There was still a month to go before departure and the project would go ahead unless the security situation worsened and the Foreign and Commonwealth Office issued another safety warning. For their part, the Working Group were ready to move ahead with the project as planned, accepting that there could well be a series of alterations determined by external circumstances. John had already indicated that he would have to return early, two days before the end of the project. Gary had taken responsibility for risk management and the ultimate recommendation to the Group about the safety or otherwise of the project. It had been agreed that the Working Group would be proactive in relation to their duty of care to the UK team. Nonetheless, Gary said he would contact each member of the party, to provide each with the opportunity to withdraw.

The postponement of the West Bank 'Rainbow' project

Other details remained to be confirmed. Although it was agreed to proceed with the project in Israel, sadly the project in the West Bank had to be postponed. This was also the decision, separately made, by the Rapprochement Centre in Beit Sahour/Bethlehem. In a communication to Geoffrey they reported that access to the West Bank was impossible due to the Israeli invasion and control. Hence, even if the WSPP wanted to attend it would not have been possible. However, the project was not cancelled, but postponed to indicate instead that it would be re-started without further delay when conditions changed to make the event possible.

David reported that the equipment for the project had already been shipped and it was agreed to make suitable arrangements with the British Council so that their office in East Jerusalem would receive and store it until it could be passed on to

Bethlehem at a suitable juncture. This meant that the coaching team would return to the UK the day after the tournament and not remain, as originally planned.

There was some discussion about the content of the Conflict Prevention and team building side of the project and Geoffrey was concerned that there should be clear understanding on all sides about the mutual aims and objectives. John, however, was less keen than Geoffrey about the production of written material beforehand. Gary wished to film the project as a record of the week to show to the donors of the equipment.

There were many dire warnings that they should not go to Israel that summer. However, against all the odds, on August 22, the project commenced. Geoffrey again kept a rough diary of events which, although incomplete, contained his perceptions on a day-to-day basis.

The Second WSPP in Ibillin, Misgav, Tivon
Daily Record, 22–30 August 2002

THURSDAY, AUGUST 22

The UK coaches met at London Heathrow in good time and there were no hitches en route. The team was met in Tel Aviv by Rami Maroun, the football coach with Agir of Ibillin. Rami was continuously with the coaches and played a splendid part in the liaison throughout. The coaches were taken to the same student guesthouse as the previous year and were warmly received by the Khoury family who owned it. The guesthouse was a wonderful place to stay because of the proximity to the participating communities and the warmth of the owners, who were obliging in so many positive ways.

The coaches had dinner in Ibillin with some of the local team, which was sponsored by the British Council and was warmly appreciated. The Mayor of Ibillin and others gave a warm speech of welcome and support and it was thought to be useful in the future to have buffet-style meals to enable fraternal mixing to take place more easily.

FRIDAY, AUGUST 23

The coaches visited the three pitches in the morning while Jane

Shurrush of the British Council took Geoffrey and John to rent a car and to oversee the transportation of the equipment from their offices to Ibillin. The equipment for the 'Rainbow' project in Bethlehem was retained, to be forwarded later at the end of September to the offices in East Jerusalem.

Rami took the team to Akko (Acre) in the afternoon where they made a tour, followed by a refreshing time on the beach. The evening was spent relaxing and Geoffrey went to visit Sohil Haj for discussions, but also found himself in a pre-wedding celebration with some 500 people in a wonderful, hectic, Arab festivity. He returned to find the team also enjoying their own festivity!

More seriously, Sohil informed Geoffrey that the celebration barbecue on the final evening had been cancelled by one of the leaders. As the team had not been told of this, Geoffrey suggested that the original host for the first Friday night, Elias Haj, who had not yet returned from a visit to Europe, might be glad to be approached instead, in order to be the host for that final occasion. However, it was seen to be essential in future for decisions to be made corporately, rather than individually without consultation, and in advance when possible, so that the principle of team work became part of the ongoing fabric of the whole operation.

SATURDAY, AUGUST 24

Sohil had arranged for the coaches to visit Lake Galilee with an excellent guide and they were given a tour of some of the historical places of religious significance. This was a time of further team building by the coaches and was noted for future years: i.e. that all the teams of coaches could enter into a day of togetherness for team building between the UK team and the three communities, prior to the work with the children. This had been envisaged and planned, but did not take place. It was noted that the coaches from the three communities were rarely present all together and, therefore, in future all coaches should be asked to participate fully and not to come and go at will. Moreover, reserve coaches also needed to be in place so that a full complement of local coaches was always present, rather than just in spasmodic attendance.

That evening the coaches prepared their own meal at ease, from the large supply of food that was delivered by Sohil. The excellence of the bonding of the UK team was largely due to the selection process of John and Gary and their *esprit de corps* became stronger as the project continued. However, it was noticeable that it did not become widespread between the three participating communities because at that stage the other coaches did not find it easy to visit each other's communities. It took another year for this to become more commonplace.

SUNDAY, AUGUST 25

The preparation meeting of the coaches took place in the offices of the Ibillin local council. This was only partly attended by the local participants, but it became energised when the coaches that were present met in small groups to plan together. Information that had been promised, such as names and numbers, was not available after all. It was important that leaders learned to deliver what they promised rather than make the promise and not deliver on it. There was some difference about the way the equipment was to be divided because Rami Maroun made the point that it needed to be divided four ways, and not three, in order to include Agir, which was a separate organisation. It was agreed to discuss this later but, at the time, the UK team did not understand the internal difficulties that had still to be addressed. The subject of transportation of Ibillin children to Tivon and Misgav became an issue. The first view was that one bus for 75 youngsters would be adequate, but this was opposed by Sohil. Geoffrey made it clear that the WSPP could not support such a practice; that there needed to be a greater awareness of safety in the transportation of youngsters in WSPP projects, and that two buses had to be available for the transport of the Ibillin youngsters. One bus alone was not acceptable and so the arrangement was eventually changed.

An excellent lunch was provided for the team by Auni and Aziza Edris in their home in Shefaram. It was a surprise, however, to find that only the UK team had been invited and that no others were present. The matter of inclusiveness and exclusiveness came up from time to time, and it became clear that this needed to be addressed and fully understood by the participants in future projects.

The afternoon saw the first games of the football project, when the buses brought children from Tivon and Misgav to Ibillin. Each group sat separately, until they were brought together. The

70

events on the field of play looked excellent and the first objective of bringing the youngsters together was achieved. However, a number of points were apparent. We were without the promised number of local coaches; it took 40 minutes to get the youngsters divided into groups because the names and ages were not available, despite assurances beforehand that they would be provided; half of the participants stayed on the field, and the other half sat on the gravel ground of the car park for the next part of the project, which was unfortunate; the entrance became flooded to an area covering some six feet due to inadequate drainage up to a depth of 3 or 4 inches so every youngster had to walk through water to get to the pitch. As Malcolm Muggeridge used to say: "It's all part of life's rich tapestry."

That evening the coaches were shown the Arab area of Haifa by Auni Edris. The initiative was fine, enjoyable and greatly appreciated, but it appeared to be in isolation, rather than inclusive of the grassroots team as a whole. Geoffrey, meanwhile, met Sohil and many of the people of Ibillin who were at the second part of the wedding celebration, with hundreds present, following the initial celebration on the Friday. The warmth of the welcome given to him by large groups of people gave an indication of the pleasure and support of the community. Good public relations were continued, if unconventional and unexpected, but all quite magnificent! Despite some early hitches, the UK team felt overall that the first day had gone very well.

MONDAY, AUGUST 26 – TIVON

The UK team was taken to Tivon in the morning and given a tour of the ancient necropolis. Lunch was taken, before which the local leaders were very supportive for the need of one of the UK team to see a doctor, and they facilitated it with warmth, kindness and concern.

The Tivon pitch in the afternoon had no shade and everyone had a long time in the sun. However, there was no shortage of enthusiasm on or off the pitch. Some mothers came to see what was happening and became worried at the sight of Arab children so close to Jewish children. Geoffrey explained what was happening and as the football continued with sounds of pleasure, the mothers relaxed and wanted to know more about the venture. Their questions of anxiety changed to questions of interest and

71

they swiftly became friendly and warm. One mother left and returned with a huge tray of home-made cakes. This seemed to be one more wonderfully simple symbol of the local response. A journalist from the Jewish Telegraph, Lydia Aisenberg, also arrived and was pleasantly surprised and very enthusiastic about the project and the concepts which lay behind it. She wanted to explore whether her community at Givat Haviva could participate next year and made firm contact with Geoffrey, which continued into the following year and thereafter with great success. Her enthusiastic commitment and participation was an ongoing encouragement. The President of the Tivon community work, Elana, also came and became increasingly activated as she saw, and appreciated, the tasks that were being undertaken. She hosted the dinner in the evening and was most warm and supportive for the events this current year and those proposed for 2003.

The UK team felt the day had been another excellent step forward, but were concerned about the non-involvement of some of the local coaches who had not appeared.

TUESDAY, AUGUST 27 – MISGAV

The team left early for Misgav and again there was no shade at the pitch, but this appeared to cause no problems. For the Social Education, the British Council had arranged for half the youngsters to see the film, *Jimmy Grimble* while the others played football, and then vice versa for the other half of the morning. Despite being enjoyable, the coaches felt that the time could have been better spent in different kinds of team work. Nonetheless it was a very good morning and another step ahead, but it might have been more; the youngsters were still not mingling, but sitting apart when they were resting.

In a late evening meeting, Geoffrey and the UK coaches were coming to appreciate that changes would benefit the project immediately, as well as in the future. By then it was a regular event to go into the courtyard of the guesthouse at night and to discuss events of the day and to share ideas together. They initiated a series of changes for the next two days in an attempt to involve them in activities which dramatically altered the dynamic the next day. They also raised a range of issues which they saw as important for the project in the future and a list was recorded.

They are included here for the sake of any manual which might be produced for future projects by others:

➢ It is considered essential to have the list of names and ages of youngsters beforehand.
➢ The local coaches were not always present, sometimes wandering off and were not always enthusiastically involved, as though they were not properly prepared and briefed.
➢ More work needs to be done on relationships because there appeared to be insufficient involvement by all the coaches, although some gave without stint.
➢ Not all the local coaches attended team building and this must be corrected by being on board throughout. Those local coaches who did attend were very good.
➢ Coaches should provide a model for the mixing of the children from the different communities by doing it among themselves.
➢ A preliminary booklet could be prepared beforehand of all the coaches for distribution so that everyone had a photo and brief outline of every coach.
➢ The first day next year should be for all the coaches to have an interactive team event such as water polo.
➢ Is the attitude of the supporting partners one of dedication, or because it is their paid job and they do not see the real point of the project?
➢ The opening dinner was appreciated but could be structured to make mixing and interaction more effective.
➢ The timetable next year could be organised so as to avoid coinciding with the Shabbat i.e. the UK coaches could leave the UK on the Saturday and arrive later in the afternoon.
➢ The Sunday could be spent on team building for the total coaching team.
➢ The project of the youngsters could be held from Monday to Thursday with the final tournament before the Shabbat on the Friday morning.
➢ A preliminary visit could be made months earlier to ensure that everything was in place.
➢ The internet could be used rather than films.
➢ The youngsters and coaches could eat together in the villages before returning home.

➤ There should be emphasis on the four way 'Buddy system' from the outset to ensure early mingling.
➤ One vehicle was insufficient for transport and a minibus or two cars should be available.
➤ All coaches should have the same strip with printed names.
➤ Youngsters should have uniform shirts, but different to those of the coaches.
➤ Blue and purple are the colours of the University of Brighton and could be used.

The coaches then continued to work even later still, to arrange a series of alternative interactions for the following day. These were to be startlingly effective.

WEDNESDAY, AUGUST 28 – IBILLIN

The morning was spent in Nazareth, visiting more of the historical, religious sites and then on to Nazareth Village which showed the city in Biblical times. This was appreciated, but exhausting, and would have been better at a different time of day due to the heat. The team was then taken to the offices of the British Council where the leaders used the resources to type and print the tournament details, while the others continued pooling ideas for next year and getting to the details of the afternoon programme.

Geoffrey and Jane continued to extend the network of support by arranging a meeting for the coaches the following day with the Anglican Bishop of the Middle East, Bishop Riah al Assal. Because of the need to plan the final stages of the project carefully on the following morning, it was later felt that this was impracticable and should be put on hold. The Bishop was then contacted and he willingly arranged to meet them shortly before he left for Cyprus the following day. When the meeting took place, he introduced them to some of his staff, including the headmaster of the school, who were enthused by the idea of the project next year.

On returning to the pitch, the field looked like several rugby matches going on at the same time. The youngsters were indistinguishable in piles of bodies as they were playing "pyramids" and other "tumble" games. When the children were separated into a variety of teams, groups and pairs, the communities became mixed, unlike earlier. This was before the football took place! It was a remarkable sight to see the participation and enthusiasm on the field as the different communities became one mass of interactive and hilarious humanity. This turned out to be by far the most successful of the Team Building, Conflict Prevention, or Social Education parts of the project. It brought youngsters together in joint, problem-solving, operations which were physical, mental, energetic and thoroughly enjoyable. The games that had been devised included an enormous amount of body contact which expressed itself in different kinds of human heaps, producing spontaneous and noisy hilarity. The whole atmosphere had changed to a more easy-going spirit of camaraderie, with lively, energetic conversation and playfulness which had not been there before. The body language and the exuberant noise said it all.

Later, Geoffrey was approached in different ways by several local coaches to change the arrangements for the evening and the planning for the tournament the following day. Gary and Geoffrey were flexible regarding the timetable, but pointed out that the local planning team had agreed and printed the programme. This was not the time for any individual or group to say that it was wrong or needed to be changed or could not be done. They nonetheless went on and accommodated the change in arrangements but, once more, it turned out to be more complex than it appeared on the surface.

The Ibillin planning team had responsibility for a barbecue that night and it was a fine and enjoyable occasion. By this time, John Sugden had returned to the UK but Geoffrey and Gary were happily present with their team. Yet hardly any of the partners arrived from the three communities, and the work was done by a few. There were matters in the air that the UK team did not understand, on which they needed time to ponder. For example, what could they learn from the world of group dynamics about the unconscious reasons for doing some things and not others? What was the modelling of the principal Ibillin Planning Team for the three satellite planning teams? Probably there was a great deal to be learned, but it all changed, or nearly all, the following day!

THURSDAY, AUGUST 29 – TOURNAMENT DAY

The morning was to be spent in joint planning for the tournament, but once again, few attended the meeting from the

75

communities. Geoffrey later chided the leadership of the absentees for their requested 'change of goalposts' and their inability to support the changes they had themselves requested. Something had been going on, which never came to light, and remained a mystery because no one was telling!

Geoffrey and Jane then went to Nazareth for their meeting with the Bishop, who had been a friend of Geoffrey's for many years. He immediately saw the point of the project and had them meet with some of his leaders. He had a school of some 1,200 children in Nazareth. He was supportive of the project and happy to become proactively involved in the future once the present project was completed and after the feed-back and debriefing. Then, if a third project could be envisaged in 2003, they could hopefully move ahead and become involved.

That afternoon, the planning and strategy of the coaches brought about tremendous excitement and enthusiasm for the final day. A variety of people from the three communities arrived to support the occasion, which was also honoured by the Deputy British Ambassador, Mr Peter Carter. The network-making continued to be productive. Dr Saul Zadka, a senior lecturer at a nearby college, with a high percentage of Arab students, came and was impressed and expressed his wish to meet the local leadership at a later date. He was put in touch with Sohil Haj. Mayors and leaders from Ibillin, Misgav and Tivon also came, including the new Director of the Ibillin Community Centre, Munir Diab. Moreover, in a short time there were three leaders of other communities interested in becoming involved in future projects: Bishop Riah al Assal of Nazareth, Lydia Aisenberg of Givat Haviva and Dr Saul Zadka.

However, the sense that something untoward was brewing came to a head in a sudden and explosive way. Shortly before the arrival of the Deputy British Ambassador, there was a serious altercation in public between two leaders in which Geoffrey had to intervene. Clearly they had a serious disagreement in Arabic, which led to them shouting at each other in front of a large group of children. Geoffrey did not need to understand the details and sharply called on them both to stop. Eventually they did so and angrily parted. One apologised to Geoffrey immediately, with a great sense of disappointment at his behaviour. It turned out that there was a separate agenda regarding the arrangements that had been made for the after-tournament festivities. The local team seemed to have made arrangements for a celebration supper, to which everyone was to be invited, and had moved ahead when, earlier, the person who was to be the host for the evening withdrew. Geoffrey, having days earlier already given the local group the go-ahead for the communal gathering at the guesthouse, confirmed that this arrangement could stand. There was clearly a complete failure of communication and one had gone ahead and made alternative arrangements, apparently without consultation. Although Geoffrey went on to speak warmly and appreciatively to the person concerned, it was not to be resolved so speedily. Feelings were still running high, and would take time to subside.

The arrival of the Deputy Ambassador gave the opportunity for introductions to be made and important conversations to take place. The Ibillin Council had provided improvements to their stadium so that it was possible for this to take place. The mixed teams of Jewish and Arab youngsters provided both enthusiasm and teamwork which resulted in a fine tournament. The trophies were awarded and the medals presented. Then came the speeches, too many and too long, but all in a good spirit of togetherness. It was later agreed that only a few should be given in future years, but that suggestion was to create dissension the next year! Auni had also instigated a number of awards to the coaches, but gave nothing to himself. Geoffrey gently chided his friend for this omission!

Prior to the evening, some visitors had indicated that it would be difficult for them to stay on after the event. However, after the tournament, people had changed their minds and wanted to stay and came back to the guesthouse with the UK coaches. Mercifully, tables of fine food had been supplied by the community in Ibillin and the dining room was filled to overflowing. The tables were occupied by Jew and Arab, Moslem and Christian. Discussion ebbed and flowed. When would be the best time of year to do it again in 2003? How can we make it better next time? Can we make it bigger? Geoffrey and the Deputy Ambassador, Peter Carter, were sitting with others at the same table. "Where in the land of Israel is this happening outside this room?", he asked the Deputy Ambassador. They looked around the overflowing room and he shook his head and smiled. "That's why you have to come again", he replied. They agreed that a team from the

UK would be assembled for 2003. They had witnessed another small miracle.

Boundaries were broken when the team left for the airport and home, as they stopped to do some shopping, despite the earlier decisions regarding security, and particularly avoiding shopping malls. Rami Maroun saw them off at Ben-Gurion airport, just as he had welcomed them when they first arrived, but it was back to the reality of normal life in the land. At one point he was aggressively accosted by the security officials, being an Arab, at which point Geoffrey had to step in. The farewells were able to proceed and the long procession through security took place. There was quietness during the return, as they were lost in the thoughts and recollections of the week, which had been quite unlike any other. They had achieved their objectives. There was a vast learning curve of some import for the future. And they had been privileged to be instrumental within it.

Conclusions

The objectives were met in full. The UK coaching team of staff and coaches was exemplary and very pleased at the eventual outcome of the project. The local planning team and coaches handled many things well overall, and there were many learning points for next year too. The assistance of the British Embassy and the British Council was substantial and greatly appreciated. The civic authorities of Ibillin, Tivon and Misgav were officially very supportive and resourceful.

In relation to the future, it was clearly learned that it needed to be ensured beforehand that criteria was drawn up, understood and agreed by all partners so that they go ahead effectively. Like the last words of the background song of their project video, the words resounded: "All together now"!

It was a humbling experience for Geoffrey and David to write letters of appreciation to the leaders, coaches and their families, as well as the British Embassy and British Council and all those who had supported the project to make it such a success:

In early September there was a brief summary report as

follows, which was sent to the supporters on the mailing list, some of which has already been stated.

MIRACLES TAKE A LOT OF WORK

➤ *There were many dire warnings that we should not go to Israel in the summer:*

➤ *It is too dangerous.*

➤ *The Jews and Arabs are hopeless to work with – they would rather kill each other.*

➤ *Jews and Arabs playing football together? You must be mad.*

➤ *Well, it was hard work to bring about a miracle; that much is true.*

➤ *We had to raise the money for the equipment and the air fares of the coaches. And a few more things such as accommodation and transportation.*

➤ *We had to find Jews and Arabs in Israel who were prepared to go to each other's towns and villages, when in other places they were bombing and shooting and terrifying each other.*

➤ *We had to find parents and communities that would allow their youngsters aged 10–14 to leave home and go unprotected to mix with people they feared.*

➤ *Plus, no football coaches in their right minds would go there to do this – look at Chelsea! (Some of the Chelsea team chose not to go to Israel for a European championship match against Tel Aviv HaPoel FC).*

➤ *You couldn't find enough money to pay them to take the risks.*

➤ *Quite right. But we did.*

➤ *Thank goodness for runners in the Flora London Marathon, who ran it to get the sponsorship to pay for most of the project; well-wishers made up the difference.*

➤ *Thank goodness for the University of Brighton sports department who asked for volunteers from their students and had to have a selection process to reduce the applications to a workable team.*

➤ *The UoB student team of eight coaches and two members of staff did come and as no one is paid for what they do, they were happy to get twice the normal rate of nothing!*

➤ *Without any payment, they took part in a project which may well be one of the most memorable things they will ever do in their lives. They gave themselves without stint.*

➤ *Over 150 Arab and Jewish youngsters did visit each other's towns*

and villages in three communities not far from Nazareth and Haifa.
➤ They did play football together, BOYS WITH GIRLS ON THE SAME SIDE! Unbelievable.
➤ They did mix up so that each team was made up of Arabs and Jews.
➤ Yes, they did sit apart the first time they met. And it is also true that at first they were very uncomfortable being in a strange situation.
➤ But they did get into team games and before the end they were fooling around and mingling and having fun like any other kids, so you could not tell who was who. Christian, Moslem or Jew? "The creed and the colour and the name don't matter."
➤ They did play football and learn about working together and being on the same side in order to achieve a common goal. They did learn to grin and laugh and cheer for each other. Parents came and were amazed enough to go home and bring back cakes galore.
➤ Community leaders and mayors and the Deputy British Ambassador to Israel did come to attend the final day's tournament. And they remained for supper until very late instead of going home.
➤ And they all said that this must happen again next year. It will.
➤ It was hard work. It was also a bunch of miracles.
➤ One day we will get to the West Bank as well. Just another miracle waiting to happen.

Reflections on the Second Project and thinking ahead to the Third

By September 20 it was possible for Geoffrey to distribute a report to the Working Group in preparation for its meeting on the 26th which paid tribute to the participants from the University of Brighton, the British Council, and the leaders in Ibillin, Tivon and Misgav. He also raised the matter of more careful future budgeting if it was to grow successfully. Later, on October 3, he addressed the criteria for the possible project in 2003. For David and Geoffrey, this was to be their third and concluding project, after which different organisations would need to be found if the project was to continue.

Caron Sethill and Jane Shurrush of the British Council had also presented helpful and creative separate written reports which focused largely on the local planning and co-ordination of the project. Their reports were circulated to the Working Group and welcomed. They recognised the success of the project in a number of ways. They also identified many of the problems which had their origins in internal relations and cultural differences.

Caron included the feedback of Sohil and Auni in her report. Their input indicated the differences in Jewish and Arab communities and some of the details that needed to be addressed, especially in relation to funding and the sharing of costs. The special divisions in the Ibillin community were different to others from the Jewish communities in terms of structure, power and finance. Although the project had been centred in Ibillin, because that was where it had commenced some years before, it could well be the case that a different venue might offer greater facilities for the development of the project.

It was clear that the British Council had considerable experience of working in Israel and had their own ways of working, and standards they expected of partners with whom they reckoned to work. For the future development of the project, it could be pivotal in bringing communities to work together efficiently and effectively and to be proactive in the creation of an ongoing and successful project. However, there were many different agencies that were to become involved and each had its own way of working. In England, the Working Group had blended into an effective culture over a lengthy period of successful interaction where teamwork and confidence in each other was of the essence. Equally, in working with the one community in Ibillin, the arrangements were simpler because of what had been successfully fashioned over a number of years. Now, for 2003, the "team" consisted of more components than before and included not one local council and community but six. Moreover there were other non-sporting, business organisations, such as the hotel which was to provide accommodation and meals, as well as those who provided transport, restaurants, venues, to name but a few. Each had their structures and ways of working and it would take time to blend those interests into an harmonious working-group where there was *esprit de corps* and competence. Each had their own lines of management which would require a way of working with sensitivity and awareness, and could not rely on lines of authority which had not been agreed and understood. The differences of opinion which could be reasonably resolved in the first year or two, could possibly turn into clashes of wills, unless handled wisely. All this was for the future, however.

Four weeks after the conclusion of the second project, the next meeting of the Working Group took place on September 26 to receive reports. The draft report was received and approved with pleasure as the objectives of the WSPP for its second project had been achieved. Appreciation for their assistance was expressed to the participating communities, the British Council and the donors of equipment, especially Arsenal Football Club and Adidas. The reports from the British Council and the local leadership were much appreciated. It was suggested that in order to improve the project in future, a set of criteria could be mutually established. This would mean that there would be mutual understanding and agreement about the details necessary for a successful operation. A visit in November or December may also be necessary. It was agreed that any difficulties experienced in the August 2002 project could be used as learning curves for the future.

It was agreed in principle that it might be possible to conduct a project in the Easter vacation, 2003. This could include a one-day team building event between UK and local coaches to be followed by a four-day project, culminating in a tournament on the fourth day. It could be known as the WSPP/Jewish/Arab Galilee Project. It could be considered whether the participating communities, without adding to the numbers overall, could be extended to include contingents from Givat Haviva, the Bishop Riah al Assal School in Nazareth and the educational community facilitated by Dr Saul Zadka. It was indicated that participating communities might be asked to cover certain costs, e.g. accommodation, internal transportation and carriage of sports equipment from the UK.

However, the 2002 budget had not been realised, there being a shortfall in money raised at the Marathon. It was hoped that the British Council might help, in addition to the University of Brighton, from whom £1,000 had been promised. For 2003, the UK fund-raising and equipment supply would be explored by David Bedford, Laurie Robinson and John Sugden. The WSPP agreed it would raise the team of UK coaches, and cover the costs of their air travel to Israel and the costs of the equipment.

Changes in the British Council in Israel

So the energy and vision were there to take the project forward for the all-important third time. But things were rapidly changing and needing adjustment. Among other things, including the extensions in Israel, the British Council itself was undergoing changes in Israel because David Elliott, the Director, was moving on and would be replaced. In October an introductory e-mail arrived from Kevin Lewis, the new British Council Director in Israel. He was clearly positive about the success of the project and its continuing development. He was also like-minded with the Working Group in terms of an effective structure becoming established, with widening scope for incorporating other organisations for its financial stability and operational success.

However, there were still problems in respect of the fund raising by the Marathon runners, which had taken place six months earlier. Money had still not been completely forthcoming and there were still bills to be paid, but insufficient funds for their payment. Geoffrey informed colleagues that the subject needed to be addressed as a matter of urgency. In relation to the budget, money was still coming in and it was going to be close as to whether the books would finally balance.

The Working Group meeting on October 16 was organised around the visit to the UK British Council of Caron Sethill. She was introduced to the members and warmly welcomed to the meeting. Caron unexpectedly gave a cheque for £350 which was the balance from the money which the British Council had allocated to the project. It was gratefully received. The recent project was discussed and it was agreed that the objectives had been achieved.

Geoffrey reported that he had sent letters of thanks to the variety of people who had helped in the project in the UK, including the families of all the coaches and the coaches themselves. It was still essential to see to small things, such as letters of appreciation and recognition, so that people felt valued and not taken for granted. This included people in positions of responsibility who were accountable to others, such as the Vice-Chancellor of the University of Brighton, Arsenal Football Club, Adidas, The British Council and the British Embassy.

They discussed the Galilee 2003 project for which WSPP had

ultimate responsibility, but had a policy of working with the grassroots communities and organisations. The date had still to be finalised but late June, rather than Easter as suggested previously, seemed to be the best for the University coaches and would be offered to potential partners in Israel. Emphasis was laid on the need for team building with the UK coaches and the local coaches on the first day, prior to work with the youngsters.

Concern was raised about the differences between the Ibillin organisation and that of the Jewish organisations. There was also concern about the difficulties that had arisen within Ibillin itself and the hope that this was being resolved for the future. The matter of numbers of youngsters would have to be considered so that the project was properly managed. Different options such as back-to-back programmes, could be considered. There might have to be a quota system if there were too many applicants. It was asked if it might be better if the project was held after school hours rather than during the day and the decision had to be made by the local communities.

The matter of financial arrangements with partners in Israel needed to be organised. The WSPP could provide the coaches and equipment and the transportation to Israel. However, it was hoped that Israel partners would cover the cost of accommodation, food and transport. It was felt to be essential that the British Council co-ordinated the project with the partners from the early planning stages and was available throughout the project.

Caron gave a summary of an earlier British Council meeting. There was a plan to bring together a number of compatible projects which could be co-ordinated by the British Council, with a paid person to undertake the responsibilities. It would work with the Israel Department of Science, Culture and Sport, together with a project board in Israel consisting of representative members from the bodies involved. Enthusiastic discussion followed, because this was in line with the policy of the WSPP to work with other bodies such as the 'Dreams and Teams' of the British Council.

It was agreed that the Galilee Project of 2003 would be pursued, with an eye to the development of the British Council initiatives and to see how there might be overlap and co-ordination in the immediate and foreseeable future. Other names were included for the Galilee project including Givat Haviva, the

Bishop Riah School in Nazareth, and one involving Dr Saul Zadka. For the British Council extension, there could be the Maccabim Association, Arsenal, Maimonides, Seeds of Peace, and World Vision. The Peres Center for Peace which worked in the West Bank was included regarding the future Bethlehem project.

For the next step, Geoffrey would invite the six potential partners to participate in a late June/early July project co-ordinated by the British Council, in partnership with the local communities. It was important to establish both the numbers they would wish to be involved and the number of assistant coaches they might wish to be included. Planning for the Galilee 2003 project was well under way.

4

The British Council and UK Universities
The Third Project, 2003

After two successful projects in successive years, was there to be a third which could demonstrate a track record for others to take forward into the future? That was the original vision of Geoffrey and David in 2000. Their intention was that this project should be one where they worked for their own redundancy. But could it be accomplished when there was so much growing violence and bitterness in the Middle East? Would they get the youngsters from even more communities? Would they get the volunteer coaches? How would it be financed when they relied on contributions to make up the shortfall between income and expenditure? There were questions galore and few answers. It was clear that the project was about to be expanded and would therefore need more careful planning. In a very short space of time, two projects had come about successfully.

To the pleasure of the co-founders, the British Council was keen to take on the organisation of the project in Israel, bringing with it their own standards. Moreover they had the resources to facilitate relationships with other bodies in Israel to enlarge the project in 2003. Geoffrey was able to confirm with John Sugden of the University of Brighton on October 24: "We are indeed working for our future redundancy." Moreover, while the project had previously centred on Ibillin now, with the extension to

86

include at least three more towns, it could likely focus on somewhere more central, like Nazareth.

Geoffrey also suggested to John that it would be useful at this stage to think of more sports colleges which might become involved for the future. The same day he contacted Jane Shurrush of the British Council to indicate that he would consult with Kevin Lewis to request that she, and possibly Caron too, be formally seconded or allowed to focus on the development of the project between now and the summer of 2003. By November 2002 it was possible for Geoffrey to contact the six potential participating communities in Israel and invite their participation for 3–11 July 2003. It was hoped that the three communities, with whom they had previously made contact in the Summer, would be included, but that did not become possible. However, the British Council was to make other contacts which enlarged the project nonetheless.

The Working Group meeting later in November was immensely significant for two reasons. The first was that Jane Shurrush had initiated connections with four other communities, to expand the project in two extra separate venues. The second was that the extension would require a larger coaching team and it was immediately agreed to act on these possibilities. David initiated informal contact with Brunel University and St Mary's College, Twickenham. It was acknowledged that the presence of the WSPP would eventually disappear if the British Council took increasing responsibility for the project in Israel, although it would gladly be supportive as the situation developed. It was seen to be a step forward if the British Council in the UK would also appoint a liaison person to work with the UK side of the project. However, it was essential for the projects to be seen as Conflict Prevention, and much more than sports development only. At the time, however, this increase of British Council liaison personnel in the UK could not be brought about.

Among the matters remaining from the recent Second Project, it was agreed, and affirmed by John and Gary, that the principles of risk assessment needed to be understood by the coaching teams, and visits to shopping malls and the use of public transport were strictly, self-imposed, exclusion zones. The matter of both acceptable accommodation and sound levels at night by the coaches would be co-ordinated by the British Council which was undertaking the responsibility for accommodation in 2003.

In terms of logistics, the Working Group expected to raise the coaching team and the necessary equipment. The cost of the air fares for a March visit and the Galilee July 2003 project itself would also be covered by the Group. It was expected at the time that the participants in Israel would cover the costs of accommodation and hospitality, internal transportation, and the shipping of the equipment. The British Council would co-ordinate the community and social programmes with the participating communities, including the age range and numbers of youngsters taking part.

In relation to the postponed project in the West Bank the previous summer, Geoffrey reported that he had made contact with the key players, namely the Rapprochement Centre in Beit Sahour, the Consul General in Jerusalem, the British Council in East Jerusalem and the Sports Department of the Peres Center for Peace. It was expected they would meet with their representatives in March. Meanwhile it was extremely gratifying that the football equipment, which had been sent in August, had been delivered to Bethlehem/Beit Sahour and was being used in the community, despite the severe conditions.

The network established over the years by Geoffrey, was again being utilised. He informed the meeting that he was exploring the idea of a second video, in addition to the one which could be produced by the University. This involved making contact with Meridian TV, as Geoffrey had previously worked until the late 1970s with the company's predecessor, Southern Television.

By January 2003, it was reinforcing to discover that the initiatives of the British Council were bearing fruit. Geoffrey and Jane Shurrush were liaising by corresponding at a rapid rate as their initiatives were taking shape. The forthcoming project looked larger than ever, with six towns, three venues and a much larger coaching team from the UK and within Israel. Geoffrey emphasised the need to ensure that participants understood that the project was the initiative of the World Sports Peace Project and was therefore focused on Conflict Prevention. Jane for her part was also involved in the quest for funds and this became increasingly important as the project grew in size and influence. The effectiveness of their liaison produced rapid understanding, adjustment or agreement, with occasional differences.

Before the end of January, David Bedford had contacted Brunel University and St Mary's College, Twickenham, of the University of Surrey, with a view to both becoming involved in the project.

The annual problem in Ibillin regarding the availability of the football pitch had surfaced once more. Moreover there was an objective problem in relation to their stadium due to the fact that there was insufficient room for the numbers envisaged at the final tournament. It was agreed that a preliminary visit had to take place for a meeting of the key players in the UK and Israel and it was arranged for the last weekend of March. In fact it was post-poned until the last weekend in May for a variety of reasons, especially security, but also because of the newness of the project for both Arab and Jewish communities, with their complexities.

Involvement with Meridian Television and the media resources of Southampton Institute of Higher Education

While the normal discussions took place regarding the timeta-bles, venues and logistics of such a large programme, another fascinating development was taking place. Geoffrey had followed up his contacts with Meridian Television in Southampton and met people who had been colleagues of his previous contemporaries of the 1970s. Instead of obtaining from them the skills to produce a significant video of the next project, Tony Wade initiated a meeting with John Barlow of the media department of Southampton Institute of Higher Education, with whom they had a direct relationship. Within the space of a few hours, Geoffrey and John met with Jim Doyle, who was in charge of the Institute's Centre for Creative Development, and it was agreed that his Centre would make the film themselves for the project and supply the personnel to do it. Although the informa-tion came the following day that the proposed visit at the end of the month needed to be postponed until later because of security difficulties, there was a creative energy in the air again because of this fresh input from Southampton, with all the excitement and adrenalin that came with it.

Other important matters turned out to be less exciting and more tedious. One concerned the painstaking detail required for the production of a brochure that was acceptable to everyone. It took a huge amount of time and energy and it was three months before it was finally produced. Even then, there had to be a separate Israeli brochure produced in their language, with their own relevant details.

It was in May that the project significantly moved ahead in terms of personnel in the UK and Israel. A Working Group meeting had been arranged for May 7, to be followed by the first familiarisation exercise of the coaching teams from the three universities. John Barlow and Jim Doyle came from Southampton Institute for their first Working Group meeting and introduced their ideas for the filming of the project, including the enlargement of their team by including Carl Dearing to lead the film crew. A number of details were then covered, including tightening up of the arrangements covering equipment, transportation, travel insurance and consent and release forms whereby the parents of children gave permission for the participation of their child in the project. Everything seemed to be going smoothly and the prospect of a visit at the end of the month was warmly anticipated. Following the Working Group, there was a gathering of the coaches in London, during which they were briefed by Geoffrey. Subsequently it was also emphasised that all the coaches had to have appropriate football coaching skills so that they could be relied on during the project.

Reconnaissance visit to Israel in May

The visit at the end of May was filled with activity. The party consisted of Geoffrey, John Sugden, and Gary Stidder, with John Barlow and Carl Dearing from Southampton and Gary Armstrong from Brunel. Their arrival at Ben-Gurion airport was unsettling because of the strange activity of Israeli security. They took three of the team and kept them in security, without explanation, for over an hour and they were only released after intervention by Geoffrey. It was strange that John Sugden and the two Garys stayed passive as they waited in the silence, cut off from Geoffrey, Carl and John Barlow. Having waited for 45 minutes, Geoffrey went to enquire about them, assuming that there had been a hold up in the baggage hall. He found that they had been detained without reason. He requested that they should be allowed to join the rest of the party. The response was largely silence and he was told that they would be coming soon. After the lengthy delay they appeared, and were very quiet. Although they professed that they did not mind and were not troubled by the experience, their demeanour told another non-verbal story. When asked by Geoffrey about whether or not they had been proactive, the fact that they said that they just waited and did not mind was an indication that they were in some kind of delayed shock which was quite understandable. Nonetheless, Geoffrey made a note to speak to the Israeli Embassy in London upon their return.

On the first morning it was warming to discover that Jane Shurrush had been successful in assembling an impressive team from the Israel Sports Authority and six partner communities in the region. Moreover, a member of the Druze community, with its Mohammedan origins, was included. The meeting was note-worthy for the warmth and friendliness around the table and the focus on creating a successful project. The logistics of the project were discussed, with the programme and the numbers of chil-dren and coaches being considered. The subject of the involvement and preparation of the local leadership was seen as essential. There was a very moving moment when Gazi, one of the supervisors of the Israel Sports Authority, described the project to the rest of the meeting in the following words: "This is the Road Map on the ground." Thereafter, Geoffrey used this phrase regularly, to describe the reality that, although this partic-ular initiative appears to have been sabotaged, the project went on to great success. The discussion even included the subject of the project in 2004 and a variety of dates were considered.

One outstanding problem each year had been the transport of the equipment, after arrival at Ben-Gurion airport. After discus-sion, the British Council was ready to receive the equipment from the UK as long as the agents of TNT would clear it from customs and deliver it to their office in Nazareth at the English Hospital. Despite this clarity and agreement, it was not to be so simple and there were still huge obstacles to overcome. For the project itself, Geoffrey and Jane would liaise and co-ordinate events before and throughout the project. Although there were inevitable blips, the preparation stage seemed largely well-achieved. The morning ended with great satisfaction around the table because of the productive nature of the meeting.

That evening the team had been invited to the annual Queen's birthday celebration at the British Embassy in Tel Aviv. The film crew ensured that, for the ongoing record, a film was taken of Geoffrey with the Ambassador, His Excellency Sherard Cowper–Coles, with the intention that more collaboration could take place with the Israeli film crew who were also present. From the outset, the team from Southampton was proactive and creative, always looking for the opportunity to record and take things forward. They were a tonic and a model for positive teamwork and yet, while alert, always low key and unobtrusive in their mode of operation. Their commitment to produce a record of excellence for the visit and the project in July was outstanding. The strategy to extend its connections, with such a strong media presence for the purposes of record and publicity, was a far-seeing activity. Moreover, the "coincidental" selection of Southampton meant that there was a film crew who could work independently, take initiatives unobtrusively and produce footage of huge value for the record of the event, which was ground-breaking, at a time of violence elsewhere in the country.

On Friday, May 30, the vision of the project, and the strategy of networking were much in evidence at the gathering at the conference centre of Kibbutz Lavi. Over 70 volunteers came for training in Football and Social Education or Conflict Prevention. Some who appeared had been in the early Knights Youth Club camps from Ibillin in 1996 and had grown and matured to be highly responsible people. This was a reinforcement of the long-term value of the projects with which there had been involvement and commitment over a number of years. Almost immediately this group of eighteen to twenty-year-olds was thrust into a carry-over from the previous year's project, as team building was to the fore at a physical level which incorporated body and brain interaction. The rooms exuded sounds of mirth and noise. Then the more detailed preparation took place for the separate teams of footballers and the Social Education groups. Meanwhile there was a separate group for the senior staff to acclimatise and understand the history of the country. The day was largely facilitated by staff from Givat Haviva, the Jewish–Arab Centre for Peace, led by Lydia Aisenberg who had met Geoffrey the previous year in Tivon. The Directors of the British Council and the Israel Sports Authority, Kevin Lewis and Dudu Malka, had been proactively supportive of the project in the weeks before the arrival of the team and were enthusiastic at the sight of its development.

In Nazareth the following day, the team was invited to meet the Mayor, his Deputy and Raji Srouji, the Sports Director and other officials. Their enthusiasm and proactivity meant that they too had caught sight of the vision and were committed to it with energy and determination. There was little doubt that the promotion of Nazareth Football Club to the Premier League in Israel, also meant that there would be sports facilities available in ways that would be profoundly influential for the future. That included the promise of the use of their stadium, pitches and resources. Subsequently, Kim Wilmshurst, who acted as liaison between Southampton Football Club and Southampton Institute of Higher Education, became involved, and there seemed the potential for exploring some fruitful twinning and interaction between the clubs and towns. However, it turned out that the success of Nazareth FC had a down turn for the project – a month after our visit we were informed that the ground would not be available because FIFA insisted that the pitch needed to be re-turfed in that period in order to be fit for international competition. A big disappointment for us, and another hurdle to be taken in our stride, but great for them!

The visits later in the day revealed some more of the gaps between the intention and the delivery capacities of some communities. Both Ibillin and the Bedouin village of Kabbiya were warm and enthusiastic about their involvement. The facilities, however, seemed short of what was required. The resources at Kabbiya needed attention to the provision of shade and proper toilets, as well as the pitch itself. Yet there was an enthusiasm to take part in the project, and the warmth of the community was impressive. Similarly in Ibillin, the facilities for the off-pitch Social Education needed to be changed as what was inspected seemed in need of substantial improvement. Leading personnel were designated to ensure that either improvement or alternative provision was made and Jane arranged for further meetings to ensure that everything would be in place.

On Sunday, the team visited the three Jewish communities.

When they arrived at Misgav, there was no longer a football pitch, but they were willing to be host to the social activities and to travel daily to Ibillin for the football. They were determined to make the project work, which revealed that a major, constructive re-thinking had gone on in a relatively short time. In moving on to the community of Ramat Yishay, the team met the Mayor and his Deputy as well as the Director of Sport who were committed to the project, despite having fewer children in the area. Their warmth and helpfulness was greatly appreciated. Only later was it discovered that they completely withdrew from the project and had to be replaced by the town of Shefaram, the reasons for which never became clear. The final visit was to Afula and there the warmth and professionalism of the local officials seemed excellent. As the pitch and buildings were situated next to each other they appeared, with Nazareth, the best prepared of all the communities.

That evening there was a reception at the home of the Director of the British Council, Kevin Lewis. The team met a gathering of like-minded people from The Peres Center for Peace, A New Way, Dreams and Teams, and The Maccabim Association. Geoffrey was suddenly called upon by Kevin to address the gathering, and he did so spontaneously which, despite his internal embarrassment, was evidently warmly appreciated.

It had been a highly successful visit in meeting and cementing relationships with colleagues, as well as ensuring that the resources were in place or would be implemented. However, there were many things that changed over the next few weeks before the actual project. In fact, on the return journey, Gary Stidder was once more taken aside and this time was searched and questioned without explanation. This was despite the fact that he carried a letter from the British Council explaining the nature of his visit, and requesting the assistance of the authorities. Again he said that he was not fazed, but it is not unusual for the shock state to include some kind of passivity and cutting off, as part of the process. It is very easy to be so taken aback by such an unexpected experience that one becomes intimidated and disempowered, and the shock factor can unknowingly kick in. So, although the matter was brushed off again, Geoffrey, on return to the UK, spent some weeks in negotiation with the Israeli Embassy for the large team in July. That team would include people who were younger and less experienced than the leadership and whose confidence could well be undermined by such an event. Eventually he obtained a letter from the Embassy especially for security at Ben-Gurion airport. This proved very helpful in July, particularly as one of the team was taken to one side; when Geoffrey noticed this, he was able to produce the document and all was well thereafter.

On their return, Geoffrey issued the following press release which would have been unthinkable only two years earlier.

"THERE ARE PEOPLE CREATING THE ROAD MAP ALREADY"

The World Sports Peace Project completed its five-day reconnaissance in Israel on Monday, June 2. It is now all set to take 20 or more staff and students from four English universities in July to its third annual Football/Conflict Prevention project.

➤ *380 Jewish and Arab children in the Galilee area will play and learn together.*

➤ *Six communities will take part from three Jewish areas and three Arab areas.*

➤ *Over 70 local volunteers are being trained to help with the project.*

➤ *The project is supported by the British Council, the British Embassy, and the Israel Sports Authority.*

➤ *The UK teams are from the universities of Brighton, Brunel, St Mary's College (Surrey University) and Southampton Institute of Higher Education.*

➤ *Everyone from the UK is an unpaid volunteer.*

➤ *A film will be made of the week-long event.*

➤ *Next year the project will be even larger still.*

➤ *The object is to enable the youngsters to learn that in order to win with distinction:*
> *they need to be on the same side*
> *they need to work together as a team*
> *they need to have the same rules*
> *they know that cheating is not acceptable*
> *they have the same set of rules and keep them*
> *they cannot shift the goalposts*
> *they do not retaliate if anyone behaves badly*

*they cannot stop the game even if someone commits a foul or
is sent off*
*they should behave like sportspersons throughout, both on
and off the field.*

**These are the footsteps of the children of today who will be
the citizens of tomorrow and who are already creating the
'Road Map' for Jew and Arab, Israeli and Palestinian.**

Count-down to the project – three weeks to go

In the following week, the Working Group met to finalise many
of the arrangements. It included a showing of the video made by
the film crew of Carl Dearing and John Barlow at the reconnaissance visit the previous week. They expected to produce this
trailer to introduce media companies to the project. Then the
documentary of the project itself would be turned into a production for distribution and an anticipated wide response. This was
to become an essential part of the project. The films, video and
CD made by Carl and his film crew meant that there was a permanent record of many parts of both the preparation and the project
itself.

A large number of supportive messages had been received.
These included greetings and good wishes from Archbishop
Desmond Tutu, Rt Hon Donald Anderson MP, Chairman of the
Foreign Affairs Committee of the House of Commons, Alan
Sefton of Arsenal FC who consistently contributed to the football
equipment and a generous gift from the Rt Hon Peter Bottomley,
the MP for Worthing, all of whom had been supportive for a
lengthy period. Southampton FC had made serious enquiries
about the possibility of sending one of their people to accompany
the team in July. St Mary's College expressed their commitment
to the project and would ensure a staff member in 2004. The staff
member from Brunel, Gary Armstrong, would have a role that
focused on evaluation and analysis as he visited the projects.

Attention then focused on the briefing day for the coaches on
June 14 at Eastbourne. The coaching team members were
confirmed by the addition of Adrian Haasner, a German student
from Brighton University, making a team of 21 in all.

Geoffrey reported on his interaction with the Israel Embassy and the events at Tel Aviv which involved Gary Stidder and two other team members. The Embassy had apologised and Jane Shurrush had expressed her feelings of anger. Although Gary continued with his assurance that, despite appearances, he had not been upset, it was agreed that such an experience should be anticipated and prevented for future teams.

The matter of equipment and its transportation was co-ordinated, with David reporting that it would be shipped on or around June 20 and TNT would provide Jane with details of their local agent. That shipment would contain the gift of footballs and cones from Arsenal FC. The medals would be coming separately from South Africa. However, "The best laid schemes o' mice an' men" prevailed. These well-planned arrangements eventually were to become seriously derailed.

Gary Stidder went through the details of the planned programme with great thoroughness. This included items concerning the pitch at Ramat Yishay, checking that the pitch for the tournament would be ready at the stadium of Nazareth FC and that the number of girls participating would be provided beforehand. It seemed that the plans were well laid and the confidence was abundant. As it was to turn out, again there was a gap between promises and delivery which caused hitches, but the arrangements so far meant that the project was well on course, despite being double in size to that of 2002 and treble that of 2001.

At the end of the meeting Laurie Robinson informed the group that he was moving to another part of the country in the summer and this seemed the appropriate time to withdraw from the group as it moved to the next phase of its existence. From around the table he was warmly appreciated for the quality of his contributions and perceptions throughout his membership of the group.

There remained the final day of preparation on June 14 at Eastbourne. John and Gary assembled their coaching team to have a day's preparation, trying out the training programme with a wonderful group of children from a local school. The following briefing was given by Geoffrey to the coaching team at the end of the day, which might serve well in any manual for similar projects:

Notes of briefing for coaching team, 14 June 2002

It is nice to think we are getting to know each other and I will keep this briefing down to three points. First, though, let me say how good it is to see you here today because we could not do this project without you. You will know that football is a metaphor for something that has wide implications: The same rules apply to everyone and no one should cheat. We have a level playing field and no one can shift the goalposts. Everyone seeks to play fair and if someone commits a foul, no one can stop the game going on. So, here are the three points:

WHERE ARE WE NOW? *Let me give some security reassurances for you and your families.*

We are in the North of Israel in a relatively non-violent area, away from Gaza and the West Bank.

We follow Foreign and Commonwealth Office guidelines and will not go if they so advise.

The Israeli security people are very strict so any one of us could be taken to one side and treated in a way that we could find difficult if we are not prepared. They will have been informed of our coming and that we have the backing of the Israel Sports Authority, the British Embassy and the British Council. Three rules:

1. Try and understand their mindset of Safety First.
2. Be polite.
3. Don't be passive – ask for me, or your leader, or the Embassy.

Be sure you have taken out a proper travel insurance.
Let me have your passport number and family home address today.

WHERE HAVE WE COME FROM? *This is the background of the World Sports Peace Project:*

We have been involved in the Ibillin area from 1994 with Arabs.

In 2000 this Football/Conflict Prevention began with David Bedford, myself and a friend from my church in Brighton who offered some footballs. It grew.

I made a number of visits in 2000 and made contact with the British Embassy–the master stroke was in asking the Ambassador to present the prizes for 2001. We also made contact soon after with the British Council at the suggestion of Mark Kelly and they were also very nice, interested, supportive and gradually became proactive and efficient – we could not have extended so effectively without them.

In March 2001 we met with Olympic Aid and by the end of the month were in touch with the University of Brighton. In only four months it was July and nine of us were in Israel with 100 children.

You can see that we are still in only our third year and you are part of the ground-breaking work of this project which has the capacity to become global.

WHERE ARE WE GOING? This is our philosophy and why we will succeed:

One of our points of genius is that so far no one is paid for what they do. Those that are involved are like you-they give their time and energy because they have the right mindset and because they are resourced elsewhere by their jobs, their families or their pensions. We need people who have a scale of mind and heart beyond the ordinary. That is why you are with us and why we will succeed.

You will see on Gary's draft programme, a brilliant last sentence: "The game is not the thing – the child is." The philosophy of this project is the even bigger picture of Conflict Prevention so that every child, of whatever age, has the right to live, feeling secure and not in danger. That is why we are together and why we will succeed.

There are terrible stories of atrocity between Arab and Jew and they live in a world of blame of others and self justification. If and when they cannot lose face and admit that maybe they were wrong, we cannot get into that, partly because we cannot understand it. We reckon to have an attitude of: "We have to move on . . . we cannot keep looking back because the future does not lie there." That is why we are able to work out there with those of similar mind and heart and that is why we will succeed.

"History is on our side." Who said that? (Fidel Castro) That is why we shall succeed; it may not be in my lifetime, but please God, in yours and you will one day be able to look back and say: "I was there and I did that."

Finally I bring you a message received last week from someone else who endured decades of racist oppression and atrocity, but who also succeeded:

Dear Geoffrey
Congratulations on the fruits of what can only be an immense amount of hard work and commitment from yourself and many others. It is indeed "marvellous in our eyes". God is good. My warm greetings to all concerned. This is wonderful. God bless you.

ARCHBISHOP DESMOND TUTU

Geoffrey added, *"Therefore, never forget, you are in very good company, and you are part of a huge and honourable tradition. And you will take this tradition forward."*

Everything that could be done had been done. The team now had to wait before going on to conduct the third project in July.

But not quite! Final details were being attended to in the week before departure. Geoffrey had to complete the liaison with the Israeli Embassy for travel, and also ensure that Gary Armstrong was clear about his role in the analysis and evaluation of the project. John Sugden and Gary Stidder were completing the finer details of the first full day's team-building with the local coaches.

But all was not well. Despite the agreement on June 29, by three Palestinian groups, for a three-month conditional cease-fire, the following day a foreign worker was murdered by the Al Aqsa Brigade. This meant the undermining of the security situation even further and the leadership wondered if worse was to follow which could mean the cancellation of the project. There were also significant difficulties for Jane in contacting key people in the leadership of Ibillin, despite the criteria laid down for partners the year before. Furthermore, Bible Lands had undergone a management change and wished to withdraw from involvement with the funds of the project, as it did not fit into the new organisation. Although this was sad because of the years of happy relationship, this was achieved swiftly and amicably.

Disturbingly, as with previous years, there were problems in obtaining the football equipment after its arrival at Ben-Gurion airport. The problem descended into a series of accusations of blame and counter blame between the parties involved. Geoffrey and the agents in London carefully avoided that process and were focused on the resolution of the problem, however it had been caused. The reasons for the difficulties could be resolved later, but meanwhile the emphasis was to obtain the release of the essential equipment. Despite the efforts of a number of people, it was an intransigent situation and, despite phone conversations between Geoffrey and the company, both in the UK and in Israel, no one seemed willing to accept responsibility for the hitch, nor could the release be obtained. As a result, the coaching team arrived in Israel without the equipment which had been dispatched weeks earlier from the UK. Eventually, after a week's delay, the equipment was released, although the project had started, but quite how that was brought about was never discovered! What we were later to find was that the bill was horrendous!

The Third WSPP, Nazareth
Daily Record, 5–13 July 2003

SATURDAY, JULY 5

The coaching team of 21 arrived at Heathrow and was given the final briefings, including instructions about the arrival at Ben-Gurion airport, Tel Aviv, and the security routines, including the letter from the Israeli Embassy. Everyone seemed relaxed and focused, despite the conflict in the country earlier in the week. As they dispersed and waited for the flight, Geoffrey had a final check-in with the leaders, particularly inviting them to include him on the list of recipients for any reports or publications about the project, for the benefit of the WSPP records or archives.

On arrival in Israel, the letter from the Embassy was shown by Geoffrey to one of the senior officials. This turned out to be fortunate because one of the group, Anthony Batchelor, was taken aside at the second check after immigration and his passport was taken from him. Geoffrey was able immediately to contact the official to whom he had spoken and Anthony, still looking bewildered, had his passport returned and was allowed to proceed with the rest of the team. However, on passing through the arrivals hall, there was no sign of the promised coach driver. He appeared half an hour later, as there had been some confusion about the time of the arrival of the flight and the arrival of the

101

team after security checks and baggage retrieval. Nonetheless, all was well, and the journey to Nazareth went without incident. Except that, despite security decisions and agreements not to visit shopping malls, there was a stop for the coaches to purchase cases of beer. It was an uncomfortable experience for certain group members, but the notion of enforcing discipline on adult volunteers seemed out of place.

SUNDAY, JULY 6
The day was set apart for joint team-building with the local volunteers and was held at a kibbutz, an hour's drive away or more, situated close to the Lebanese border. Geoffrey welcomed the group of 45 local coaches who, with the UK team, amounted to a team of 66 lively colleagues. Another indication of hitches in the local arrangements was the non-arrival of the team from Afula until after lunch, having appeared so keen only a few weeks earlier. As it turned out, their support and input was significantly short on what had been promised and expected. This was a disappointment and was possibly down, again, to changes in personnel, and people with different responsibilities. Apart from that, the day was full of energy and enjoyment, with people working hard together. More attempts were made during the day to obtain the equipment, including phone calls to and from the UK, but to no avail. Earnest concern was expressed, with every good intention but still the intransigence was maintained somewhere in the system.

Excellent exchanges of ideas took place between Geoffrey, and Gazi and Omar of the Israel Sports Authority. These focused on the pitch for the final tournament because the promise of the use of the facilities of the Nazareth FC had been withdrawn because of the requirements of FIFA to have the stadium and its resources upgraded for the matches which would be played in the Autumn. This was one more disappointment that had to be taken in one's stride. There was no point in wasting energy with blame and grievance when the primary task was to find an alternative resource – fast! This was not easy but the tireless work of Gazi Nujidat and Raji Srouji eventually produced an alternative venue. This had proved problematical, but finally one was found, although the standard of the replacement pitch was very disappointing. Nonetheless there was no question, as far as the two

Filming the coaching of the coaches. Preparation day for Jewish and Arab assistant coaches prior to the Third Project, July 2003.

Final Tournament Prize-Giving – Third Project, Kfar Tavor sports ground, July 2003. British Ambassador His Excellency Sherard Cowper-Coles presenting a medal to a team member, watched by hundreds of Jewish and Arab players, coaches and spectators.

Final Tournament Prize-Giving - First Project, Ibillin sports ground, July 2001. Refreshment time – left to right: Sohil Haj, Leader of the Knights Youth Club, Ibillin; British Ambassador His Excellency Francis Cornish; Atif Haj, Mayor of Ibillin; and members of the Ibillin Council.

Mixed Jewish and Arab teams assembling at Bedouin sports ground, Kabbiya Village, July 2003.

Opening Day at the First Project, Ibillin sports ground, July 2001, with the Arab village of Ibillin in the background.

Honorary Citizenship Award of Ibillin, 10 November 2001. Mayor of Ibillin, Atif Haj, making a presentation to Geoffrey Whitfield, with Sohil Haj, Leader of the Knights Youth Club.

Final Tournament
Prize-Giving – Third
Project, Kfar Tavor
sports ground, July
2003. Left to right:
British Ambassador
His Excellency
Sherard Cowper-
Coles, Geoffrey
Whitfield and Raji
Srouji, Director of
Sport, Nazareth.

Third Project, Ibillin sports ground, July 2003. Mixed teams of Jewish and Arab
youngsters.

UK Team Departure,
Heathrow Airport,
London, for Second
Project, August 2002.
Left to right: Gary
Stidder, Senior Coach,
Helen Goodacre, Sharon
McSwegan, Eamon
Brennan, James Scott,
Chris Howarth, Naomi
Poletyllo, Simon
Hinchcliffe, Steve Smith
and John Sugden,
Deputy Head, Chelsea
School of Physical
Education.

leaders from the Israel Sports Authority were concerned, that there would be another project in 2004.

That evening, after a very successful day for those who had been present, there were plans to be made for the rest of the week, especially the Final Tournament itself. It had been agreed the previous year that there should be a limit to the number of speeches and, despite Jane's misgivings about people being insulted if they were not invited to give a speech, the agreement was kept and only Geoffrey and the Ambassador would give short speeches. However, the lunch afterwards, hosted by the British Council, would give the chance for anyone to make a speech if necessary, including all the local mayors. In the event, none came to the tournament or to the celebratory meal. Another strategic decision concerned the need for a full debriefing at the end of the tournament and before departure. It was agreed that this would take place on the Sunday morning before the brunch with everyone involved expected to attend, so that discussion could include strategy, learning points, policy, dates, and a development strategy for the future.

Before departure, it was made clear that, despite the meeting only a month earlier with the mayor and some of his staff, the Jewish community of Ramat Yishay would not take part, because they had only a few children available at the time. Geoffrey strongly emphasised that they should be invited to bring a number so that they did not feel excluded, even if it amounted only to one car load of youngsters. Despite this, no one came from the community. It was still difficult to come to terms with sudden changes in arrangements without explanation or any statement of regret, let alone an apology. It was as though the previous meetings and arrangements, made with pleasant, warm contact had never taken place. Projects from abroad have much to learn about different mindsets in different countries. In some places, apologies are difficult because it is interpreted as a fault, which involved a loss of face, rather than a regrettable event from which all might learn and move on. However, their part in the project had been taken by the Arab community of Shefaram. They were welcome, but this meant that there was an unexpected change in the planned ratio of participation because now there were two Jewish communities to four Arab communities.

By late morning there was still no sign of the equipment. Eventually there was a phone call from TNT in the UK still arguing about whose responsibility it was to handle customs in Israel. Geoffrey suggested that inquests about responsibility would be important later, but the essential issue was the delivery of the equipment. The coaches left for their designated venues, again without any equipment. However, at 2.30 in the afternoon, a lorry arrived! Footballs, shirts, cones and bibs a-plenty. It was not then realised that one essential item was not there – the medals!

Meanwhile the coaches that were travelling to the Bedouin village of Kabbiya had got lost because the driver had neither map nor travel instructions. Despite the request for maps, these were not provided and throughout the project it became a problem for the drivers, especially coming home at night in the dark. Fortunately it became a daily joke in the team, to the point of hilarity, rather than a crisis. It revealed a positive attitude in the team, when elsewhere there was a tendency to blame others and so avoid guilt, which sometimes seemed to be part of the prevailing culture.

In visiting the Social Education input that afternoon in Ibillin, both Caron and Geoffrey were concerned about difficulties they were experiencing with the Misgav and Ibillin youngsters. There seemed a lack of expertise in working with children, including issues like control and leadership, and the same appeared the case in the Afula and Nazareth combination. This was probably inevitable for the project, and what was required was openness about the difficulty, so that it could be learned from, rather than instigating blame and excuses. This seemed to be a regular occurrence in a number of different and unconnected situations. The youngsters seemed unfazed by it all, but it did not seem to be going according to plan. That particular attitude of 'learning curves' instead of 'blame' seemed an essential pattern for the project in future years. Interestingly, the Social Education programme in the Kabbiya – Shefaram pairing seemed satisfactory – and these were two Arab groups, although Bedouin and Arab have their own differences also, but on a different set of values.

That night the team was invited to the Bedouin village of

Kabbiya which was a memorable event for the setting beneath the stars and the wonderful hospitality – and the journey home. Again there were no maps, and the vehicles travelled through the dark, making their separate journeys home, arriving back very late, but all in the best of humour.

TUESDAY, JULY 8
The coaching team went in their cars around Lake Galilee, and visited some of the significant Biblical sites, including the place of the Sermon on the Mount, on the Mount of Beatitudes situated looking over Lake Galilee, which stretched out before them. Geoffrey introduced the notion of the 'Blessings' sayings of the Beatitudes being also a set of profound political statements during a time of foreign occupation, and that it might be related to the current situation. He suggested that the team might imagine Christ saying to the Israeli Defence Force or Hamas, or to Sharon and Arafat: "Blessed are the poor in spirit . . . Blessed are the meek . . . Blessed are the merciful . . . Blessed are the peace-makers" etc. It provided a different perspective for consideration. They then went on visiting other sites around the lake, and particularly took time at a place, remarkable for its stillness, named Mensa Christi, where it is recorded that Christ met his disciples after the Resurrection. A few days later, the coaches were by another part of the waterside and saw the way the lake was very quickly turned into a storm so dangerous that everyone had to get out of the water at speed. They finished up at the Ron Beach hotel where they had lunch and spent time relaxing on the beach and swimming in the lake before returning refreshed to the project.

During the journey, Jane informed Geoffrey of her strong feelings because he had not followed the instructions of the British Council which wanted assurances that it would have editorial rights over the filming distribution. Geoffrey explained that he was unable to give a promise which he could not deliver and that it was a matter that he and Carl Dearing, as head of the film crew, had yet to discuss, but it had been flagged as an item for discussion. This was not the expected response and the British Council seemed to take a much heavier view of the matter. As the project was less than half-way through, there was ample space for this to be resolved in unhurried time when it was not at all urgent at that moment. That kind of intensity of interaction showed a difference in attitude and culture, which had its strengths and weaknesses. It was to reappear later.

That afternoon, while the football part of the programme was extremely successful, the Social Education was in the very early days of management and 'learning curves'. In the location at Misgav, it was very difficult to locate the venue for the programme and when it was found, the numbers were unbalanced and the sessions very brief. There was a need, as elsewhere, for more experienced leadership and supervision, because these were early days for such an enterprise. Simply put, some leaders were more experienced than others. There were more questions than answers and clearly, on all sides, the project did not have the expertise to produce a successful outcome, and it needed far more external help than had first been realised. The concept was excellent, but the means to achieve its aims were in the experimental stage. If that could be acknowledged, then it would be possible to move on creatively by bringing in outside experts to enrich the programme. However, it was not simply a matter of application. There was also the more basic matter of philosophy and how much those involved really understood the objectives of the project. It also became clear that some of those involved expected payment, and did not have the mindset of the volunteers who did the work because it was a good thing to do in its own right. Hence, not everyone involved stayed beyond the fixed time to mingle and create a *camaraderie*. This is not to describe a fault, but rather a gap in communication and understanding. It was an indication that certain matters could not be taken for granted, which included the need to ensure that all local volunteers had the appropriate mindset. This would involve far more careful selection and preparation of future volunteers. As one of the local leaders smilingly said later: "The word 'Yes' has many different meanings for Jews and Arabs!" It was possible to hear echoes of someone once saying: "Let your 'yea' be 'yea' and your 'nay' be 'nay'!"

As this part of the programme was in the hands of the local people, it seemed essential that the British Council and the Israel Sports Authority should have a fresh strategy for the future on this subject. This would mean a training programme which began with the current leadership and then passed to the younger leadership. Overall skilled leadership would be strategically essential, so that trained people emerged over time, to lead and supervise this part of the work.

But it would not be easy. A second set of sessions began later and other issues emerged. The setting played a part in the ambience, so that where youngsters were in a gym, and that location was one that was associated with movement and energy, the participants became a very lively group who were difficult to lead or control, as compared to the group on the grass outside. Interestingly, the unruly groups did not have a female leader, while the others did. The overall effect was that Jewish and Arab groups sat apart during a rest period and there was no inventiveness by the leaders to deal with this. There was a great deal of what was perceived as disobedience in some groups with some leaders. Those with a background of mixing with others, such as one pair of leaders from Ibillin, seemed to have more grasp and cohesiveness with their mixed group, despite their own youthfulness. What some leaders might not have expected was that discipline and control would be such strong issues. That needed exploring as a matter of urgency for the future, because the project was not prepared for that set of agendas.

Dinner that evening, as guests of Misgav, involved another journey through the wilderness for the drivers, all in good heart. The coaching team arrived back at the hotel somewhat late and not at all in convoy, but all in one piece. The football side of the project had gone very well and morale was high.

HALF WAY REVIEW FOR REFLECTION ON A 'FEAST OF LEARNING'

That night Geoffrey, at the half-way stage of the project, compiled a list of points for consideration and evaluation as well as for future policy of this or any organisation:

Any participating community would need to have certain infrastructure in place, e.g.:
➤ A mental sub-structure which understood the philosophy of Conflict Prevention
➤ A skilled leadership sub-structure, with proper training for assistants

➤ An infrastructure with appropriate facilities and resources
➤ A proper accountable financial sub-structure

The Conflict Prevention or Social Education:
➤ Needed to be part of the fabric of that community
➤ Needed to be more sophisticated in attitude and application
➤ Could perhaps become more integrated within the football part of the project
➤ Could create innovative forms of training within the communities

Resources:
➤ The British Council could provide an extra person to work with Jane and attend to details, so that Jane might have the opportunity to exercise more of a strategic overview and therefore be less immersed in detail
➤ The costs of the organisation of the project in the UK by the World Sports Peace Project need to be included in the financial structure of future projects, rather than being carried by the personal resources of one individual

Scale:
➤ The need to focus on the bigger picture, as and when things go wrong
➤ The project is bigger than a sports project
➤ Problems like transportation of equipment, hotel limitations, lack of maps, personal disagreements are, relatively, 'small stuff'.

WEDNESDAY, JULY 9
At breakfast Geoffrey asked Gary Armstrong to focus specifically that day on his role as analyst and evaluator of the project by going to Ibillin and Misgav with the teams, visiting the Social Education projects and providing his expertise during the feedback. This was to be the crucial learning curve for WSPP for the week. They discussed the training of the Social Education coaches and Gary suggested there could be certificates to indicate those that had reached a level of expertise. The idea emerged that the British Council might be asked to organise a training group in the UK for such people, prior to the project in 2004. Moreover, that in

2004, the team might include a specialist in social studies who could guide that part of the project. Geoffrey emphasised again that there should be avoidance of blame, or scapegoating, when things went wrong, in order to create the 'feast of learning'.

Geoffrey spent the rest of the morning ensuring good relationships with the hotel staff and management. They had been very flexible, because each night the coaches took over the bar completely, bringing their own supplies of beer, and no surcharge was made. There was a separate group also using the premises at the same time, and the bar was not always left as desired, while use had also been made of the coffee machine. However, there were strong feelings about the daily breakdown of assurances that the international phone line would be connected and at one point Jane threatened to remove the entire team from the hotel. It was some time before the phone company fulfilled their promise with the hotel to connect the line so that calls could be made home. Geoffrey and the rest of the leaders had quite misjudged how important the phone was for the morale of the team. All parties agreed that there was a considerable difference in the atmosphere when they provided information for each other in a friendly way, as distinct from others who might make complaints with hostility. It was essential that the team felt at ease in a different environment and so rapport with the hotel management was important to establish, maintain and not to be taken for granted. It seemed to be essential to treat people with courtesy and dignity, whatever had gone wrong or been misunderstood. It would have been all too easy to get cross, or even angry, but one essential factor was the way we conducted relationships rather than trying to exert authority over others.

Later, however, there was a typical 'student rag', except that it went rather pear-shaped! Gary Stidder reported that his belongings had been taken from his room, including his laptop and other valuable items. It was a very sensitive situation because the UK team had largely related very well to the hotel staff and management, despite the lack of telephone facilities. Geoffrey went with Gary to check the room and then to see the management, making it clear that there were no accusations, simply a need to discover if the equipment had been moved to a place of safety. The management took it extremely seriously and interviewed the domestic staff. The General Manager came on the

113

scene and was very stern, even though Geoffrey was clear with him, too, that there were neither complaints nor accusations on the part of the team. On returning to the room with the General Manager, who was looking extremely intense, two of the coaches stood by their rooms, chuckling and looking extremely innocent. Immediately the penny dropped! Gary had been on the receiving end of a 'student rag'!

The General Manager was furious and spoke his mind in no uncertain terms. Geoffrey had to intervene and agree that the matter was out of order, and should be left with him to deal with. The mixture of emotions was kaleidoscopic. A harmless prank had seriously backfired, and the only way to deal with it was to acknowledge it, with appropriate apologies made by the students to all concerned, not least the domestic staff. The ringleaders wrote and delivered a letter of apology, while Geoffrey spoke first to the manager, Samir, and then the General Manager, Hoosama, thanking them for their professional attitude to the problem. It was fortunate that earlier in the day, Geoffrey had spent time building bridges between the project team and the management! Perhaps the issue of student humour does have national and cultural boundaries, but, for a while, it was a very tricky situation. Gary and his possessions were soon restored to each other, and the day continued.

Jane still had strong feelings, remaining from the previous day, over the editorial rights of the filming by Carl and the Southampton film crew. Geoffrey took a softer line and indicated that it could easily be discussed later, together with Kevin Lewis. Jane, however, earnestly wanted a signed letter immediately. Being present, Carl offered to sign such a letter as he was the film-maker. The way of settling differences between colleagues seemed beyond all proportion, especially when there was every intention of finding a happy, common agreement during the course of the week. There were obvious differences in style between the two; one who needed the problem fixed immediately, perhaps because of instructions from elsewhere, even if it could not be so fixed, and the other who took a more relaxed, and less head-to-head stance, because it would be resolved with goodwill.

In the afternoon and evening, it was more of, "the best laid plans o' mice an' men". The teams had become mixed up in

114

Nazareth and the wrong youngsters were in the wrong place but everyone seemed fine about it! In the Bedouin village of Kabbiya, there was the feeling that the project was working well, with the coaches and youngsters happy and connected. It had become a general order of the day that when problems arose, they were there to be overcome, and not turned into a crisis. As always, blame was not cultivated, and the more creative model of human relations could thereby be cultured. This proved to be important on a daily basis.

The evening was spent in the restaurant of a potter in Nazareth; John Sugden was almost run down by one of the cars as he attempted to direct the driver into the correct turning – no maps again, just one scared driver, but not John! Rather strangely, when Geoffrey asked for the feedback from the anthropologist, the colleague said he did not want to be seen as a 'fifth columnist' and the report was never provided. Later it turned out that those responsible for the Social Education programme in Misgav had abandoned it altogether, without reference to the leadership. The learning curve richly demonstrated the need for a more thorough selection, training and supervisory system in the future leadership both from the region and the UK.

THURSDAY, JULY 10

At breakfast, Geoffrey asked Gary Stidder about the medals for the Final Tournament the following day. Both became aware that they had not seen them amongst the equipment and went to check, but they were not there, nor on the inventory. Geoffrey recalled that David Bedford had said they would come from South Africa and he immediately phoned David in London. David, for whom it was still before the day's work had started, said he would need to check and would phone back in three hours' time. Geoffrey already had to brief the team in the morning and, after he had informed them, he re-affirmed the principle of the non-punitive, non-blame attitudes behind 'learning curves' and the 'feast of learning'. John remarked to the group: "That was 'Thought for the day'!"

Geoffrey and Jane immediately combined to create an effective Plan B. It was not going to be the case that the youngsters would not have their presentation medals from the British Ambassador the following day. By 11.30 am Jane obtained some samples of medals from a local supplier in Nazareth. They agreed on the inscription, 'WSPP Galilee Project 2003' and Jane phoned the supplier with the order for 300 medals, to be ready that afternoon. Flexibility was the order of the day and Geoffrey cancelled his visit to Kfar Tavor to see the pitch for the Tournament the following morning. Meanwhile, that evening the team was to be hosted for dinner by the town of Afula. However, no one from Afula had contacted the team to inform them about the venue! At 1.15 pm David Bedford phoned from England to say that the company in South Africa had got the wrong date for delivery and thought the medals had to be ready for a month later. Geoffrey told him that they had already activated a Plan B for a supply of medals. Almost immediately afterwards, Jane phoned to say that the medals would be delivered to the three venues and she would collect them at 4 pm that afternoon in time for the knock-out part of the competition that day, prior to the finals the following day.

Geoffrey went to the pitch in Nazareth for the quarter finals in the afternoon, but Jane phoned him soon after his arrival to ask him if he would do her "the greatest favour" – would he collect more ribbons for the medals as they did not have sufficient material! With one of the helpers named Hoosama, they went into Nazareth to get the supplies. They went from one shop to another. Then more phone calls on the mobile from Jane to Geoffrey, asking: "Would you, could you, please also collect the medals?" The ribbons were purchased, but there were no dark blue colours so they accepted black, the medals were collected, then threaded and knotted, all 300 of them. Geoffrey and Hoosama finally got back to the Nazareth pitch at 7 pm, by which time everyone had gone home! But there was no chance for Geoffrey to relax as another phone call came from Jane, urgently asking him to go to the theatre in Afula where there was a special performance, and he was supposed to be a special honoured guest in view of his position as Executive Director. He made it 15 minutes from the end and was warmly greeted. Courtesies had been observed – just! The meal afterwards was delightful and, again, exuberant. Just one more delightfully exhausting, but successful, day.

FRIDAY, JULY 11 – TOURNAMENT
It was the start of the Jewish Sabbath at sundown, and so the

tournament took place in the morning in the stadium of Kfar Tavor. The pitch had been decided upon very late in the day because the other pitches were not available. There was a feeling that other issues were in the air, but it was not the time to discuss it. It turned out to be seriously deficient in terms of playing surface, toilets and facilities. But there was shade for some hundreds of youngsters who arrived to participate and watch. The Japanese media was present and they interviewed a variety of people. Kevin Lewis of the British Council, with Caron Sethill and Jane Shurrush, wanted to have a meeting with Geoffrey before the arrival of the British Ambassador although the only available venue was a changing room, next to the toilets!

The meeting covered a wide range of important issues. However, it was strange that, once more, the subject of the British Council having editorial authority over the film making was raised in a less than mutual way. Clearly there was another agenda, but it was difficult to pinpoint. For Geoffrey, it had stopped being an issue days earlier and was directly between the British Council and the film crew from Southampton Institute. For him, there were more important matters to air and to discuss. There had hitherto been a mutual, relaxed approach to problems, and an ease in discussions, but something had changed in the atmosphere and a more authoritarian approach to differences seemed to emerge, which was foreign to the WSPP mindset. Perhaps the British Council had another issue but, if so, it was not openly discussed. With hindsight, the British Council may have unconsciously assumed that the project was theirs to control when, in fact, they had been only on the periphery of the 2001 project, and eighteen months after it had commenced. It did not seem important to draw this to their attention because their involvement began to be formalised for the 2002 project. WSPP meanwhile saw them as great colleagues, as they became increasingly involved from then on. It seemed reasonable that they could be included in the team which might take over the helm, and such proved to be the case. Possibly the change in BC leadership had also been significant, but flexibility rather than rigidity, would have been a more important model for them to demonstrate to the two communities we were attempting to serve.

Perhaps, however, the issue was also something connected to expectations, authority, power and control. Many organisations function well on the basis of mutuality of philosophy and vision, where there are unspoken agreements about the ultimate goals of a project. This provides for a fertile, imaginative creative interaction, where the emphasis is on moving ahead on the basis of mutual trust and flexibility. Then the experimental, learning process can be constructive, unfettered by fear of error and hostile consequences because all are involved in the learning curve. Other organisations function well where there is a fixed structure and where authority and power involves obedience to the requirements of a senior executive body. These two ways of working are not likely to be compatible for very long unless there is clear understanding of ways to work together. This requires careful consideration and respectful discussion between the major players. In the fluid energy of the project, which had come so far in so short a time, such discussion had not taken place. The differences were coming into view while there was a project to complete. Flexibility on the one hand and rigidity on the other had possibly become an irritant and could even become an obstacle. More importantly at that moment however, some hundreds of youngsters were at the sports stadium and ready for their tournament.

On a range of other items, however, agreement was reached, including the visit of a team coming to the UK for a week of preparation to be held at the University of Brighton, the BC willingness to cover the UK office expenses of Geoffrey, and the need for greater care in the preparation of a project in 2004. In relation to future projects, it was further agreed that Geoffrey's points concerning criteria for future partners, especially philosophy, finance, leadership and facilities, had to be emphasised. It was particularly aired that the project could develop beyond the Galilee area, and extend to the South in Jaffa and elsewhere. Before ending and moving to the tournament, Geoffrey and Kevin agreed that changes in the structure of the project could be brought about, in order to deal with its future development. The improvement of the Conflict Prevention, or Social Education programme, seemed by far the most important subject for discussion. The absence of girls was also a strategic matter for the future success of the project and had to be noted for further discussion.

Meanwhile, that day the film crew from Southampton had filmed two of the lads in football kit. They faced the camera and one said: "I am Jewish", the other said: "I am Arab". Then together they said: "We like to play football together. We are friends." They put their arms across each other's shoulders and grinned. It was a moving piece of filming – a symbol of three years' work. In the stadium there was a glorious atmosphere as hundreds of youngsters cheered their teams throughout the morning. There were two sets of teams: one named after countries, which was won by "Switzerland", and the other named after Premier League teams, which was won by "Chelsea". After a short speech by Geoffrey, the British Ambassador, His Excellency Sherard Cowper-Coles, gave a brilliant speech, summarising the project and congratulating all those who had brought about the project so successfully. He then presented the cups and individual medals to a host of youngsters, who were still full of energy and pleasure. Despite the blips and hitches, the project had, for the third time, been wonderfully successful, finishing on a high. There was a match between the UK Coaches and a mixed team of local coaches from the Arab and Jewish communities. By the time they finished, both sides were exhausted and the outcome is still undecided!

The British Council hosted a lunch for everyone involved and over 100 people sat down for energised discussion about its success and how to move it forward. Geoffrey had organised a large bouquet of flowers and presented them to Jane Shurrush because of all the work she had put in so effectively over a very long period. Geoffrey asked the coaches to meet in the evening and record their positive and negative recollections so they could be collected and used for the future.

SATURDAY, JULY 12
The coaches were taken for a day's recreation to Luna Park on Lake Galilee. It was interesting to see the placid lake suddenly, in a few minutes, develop into a storm, with waves that made bathing and boating impossible. It was strange that at one point, Jane again attempted to bring pressure to bear on Geoffrey, this time by insisting that he should be present at the meal in Ibillin that evening because, if he did not attend, some would be insulted by his absence. It seemed to make no difference that he gladly intended to be present, but arrangements had also been made for him to meet some of the pioneers of the projects in the previous

119

three years, and before. It was a strange pressure to have to meet, and then to handle the demands diplomatically. It was odd to encounter once more an authoritarian attitude, which was in such contrast to what had prevailed in discussions in the UK. It proved unnecessary, because comically, those dignitaries did not appear anyway, and it became one more delightful evening! But something else was going on which was not immediately detectable, and one could only guess. Why would very nice colleagues behave so out of character and out of partnership role? Why would they use confrontation, coercion and pressure, and then become so offended when it was resisted? Perhaps they always operated like that within that culture and expected to be obeyed? Or perhaps they were used to taking over a project, rather than one in which the executive control was elsewhere, as was the case with WSPP. Their way of operating was foreign to what had prevailed for the previous three years. Hitherto, differences of opinion had always been accepted as part of strong minds harmoniously working together in a collaborative spirit.

However, if this piece of writing is meant, among other things, to be some kind of a manual for other project leaders working in the Middle East, it points out that it always involves working with factors that are not always as clear and up front as might be desired. It can be part of different personalities working together, from different disciplines and cultures. Although in this case it usually worked extremely well, it was not always easy. Certainly the WSPP had been created in a way that was professional and expert, but also had a relaxed and warm interpersonal way of collegial operating, and this has been alluded to elsewhere in this story. It was apparent that there was a clear difference between the ways the WSPP and the BC related to the hotel management and to the local community leaders. In the UK it had been successful in producing a unique project, without going through other more formal and structured channels, to which others might have been more accustomed. If that had been the case, it could well have been that the WSSP would have remained solely a committee rather than developing into a proven, successful endeavour ready for even greater development.

It has to be mutually appreciated that, inevitably, there would often be significant differences between formal, established bodies which have to relate to other such bodies, and those which are less formal, and can be more dynamic and spontaneous because they are less accountable to other agencies. There are significant differences between organisations which work with the authority model of "top-down" structures and those which function better with a "bottom-up" process. Such issues need to be recognised and appreciated, if they are to be understood and not become an impediment.

SUNDAY, JULY 13

Sunday morning was the time set apart for the leaders' debriefing. Eventually most, but not all, the leaders from the participant towns arrived, which was another example of differences in understanding and teamwork. Geoffrey opened the meeting by expressing his appreciation to everyone present. He acknowledged the fine leadership from the groups in the UK, the Arab and Jewish communities in Israel, the British Embassy, the British Council and the Israel Sports Authority. He thanked them for their skills, their warmth and friendship, and their commitment. It was their commitment to the future that made the difference in the land between those who looked back and those who looked forward. He concluded with a verse from a poem, which seemed to express something they all shared:

"We see in vision fair,
A time when evil shall have passed away,
And thus we dedicate our lives,
To hasten on that blessed day."

A wide range of items was then discussed. There was general concern about the difficulties in the Social Education programme. It was agreed that this programme should be incorporated into the team building of the football project and the University of Brighton planned to prepare a manual for use in 2004. There was also general agreement that there needed to be a long-term strategy for the football side of the project. This would include the involvement of girls, the purchase of equipment in Israel and the possible visit to the UK in the spring by a team of assistant coaches.

In terms of the planning in the region, each participating town should have a dedicated co-ordinator so that inside each com-

121

munity, people could understand the aims and prepare properly for their success. Each town should make their commitments in writing regarding the involvement of personnel, resources and finance. Meetings of the responsible people should be held on a regular basis as a matter of commitment. Then they could discuss how to take the project forward for the rest of the year, instead of it being for one week a year only. Moreover there should be a steering committee, with appointed members from the British Council, the Israel Sports Authority and each participating community. The facilities should be up to acceptable standards and not as the pitch that had been used for the tournament. Debriefing at the end of the project was also essential, and this could take place with all in attendance, rather than a day of recreation.

At the end of the session, Geoffrey checked with the two leading members from Nazareth and the Israel Sports Authority, Raji Srouji and Gazi Nujidat. Both were delighted that the meeting had gone exceptionally well, and was essential for the preparation of the 2004 project which would begin almost immediately. After brunch together the team took leave of their friends, and the journey home was quiet and uneventful.

Geoffrey again sent letters of appreciation to all who had contributed to the success of the project, not least the families of the coaching team. In the following month, others also made contributions, which largely centred on the future developments. He circulated the following report, which is repetitive in part, but also seminal for the benefit of future projects elsewhere:

Learning points and the future

The Social Education or Conflict Prevention part of the project had a range of responses between success and difficulty. It was felt that it would be better in future years to include it within the overall football training in terms of leadership and team work. The leadership from Brighton, John Sugden, Gary Stidder and John Lambert, were asked to work out a programme. They immediately saw principles which they could prepare and test by creating a manual of exercises and activities to be of use, not only for the WSPP in Israel but also as a contribution more generally to football and the wider world of sport. In conjunction with the British

122

Council, the viability of a team of coaches coming from the participating communities to the University for a training week for any 2004 project could be discussed.

Any expansion in 2004 in the Galilee area needs to be more carefully selected and organised so that certain structures are agreed upon as essential for any prospective partner. The details need to be established by the creation of a local steering committee, led by the combined initiatives of the British Council and the Israel Sports Authority, working with the local communities. The inclusion of girls in the project was essential. Four possible principles were outlined for partner communities:

> they would need to understand the co-existence philosophy of the project beyond football;
> they would have to select and maintain their dedicated leadership before, during and after the project so that reliable consistency was ensured throughout, with each community having their own internal 'steering committee';
> they would need to have the structure, facilities and resources;
> they would need to give written financial promises to guarantee their part in the project.

Expansion beyond Galilee can be explored, particularly in Jaffa, following suggestions from the British Council. There is also the commitment to Beit Sahour in Bethlehem which could not be followed through in 2002 but might be undertaken if political considerations permitted that to be planned. It may well be important for the WSPP to make an exploratory visit in November to see how these expansions and any others in Galilee could be developed. It is recognised that the West Bank has different relationships with the British Embassy and the British Council and both had been separately developed in 2002. The issues of funding and teams from the UK universities would need to be explored before then.

Final tournament. There were significant flaws in the process of pitch selection this year, and a less than adequate pitch was provided at the latter part of the week. It is to be hoped that the resources of Nazareth FC in 2004 can be used, where a fine pitch and facilities are on hand. Resources must also include proper First Aid personnel and equipment.

The visits to Lake Galilee on the Tuesday and Nazareth on Wednesday were appreciated. In 2004, there may be the need to move on to a separate venue at the end of the Final Tournament.

The lack of adequate detailed maps meant that there was significant difficulty in finding one's way around the various venues, particularly after dark.

The transportation of equipment by TNT had become increasingly frustrating in the week before departure from the UK. Despite daily interaction between the WSPP and the TNT London office, the equipment was not delivered until the Monday afternoon after our arrival and the project was well under way. It was properly distributed and used on the Tuesday. In future, to avoid this transportation difficulty every year, we should consider the local purchase of equipment.

The hotel accommodation in Nazareth was, overall, greatly appreciated by the UK team. The major hitch was the failure of the phone company to connect the payphone at the hotel despite daily requests by the hotel management. The management was especially patient in relation to the almost exclusive, nightly takeover of the bar by the coaches. Their forbearance over a prank that went seriously wrong was handled by them with a professional attitude. The UK and hotel leadership related well, despite imperfections in the daily organisation. The outcome was an expressed wish by the coaches to return there, with the expectation that some details would be improved.

The inclusion of the film team from Southampton Institute was an asset in giving a perspective as well as a record for current use and for the archives. In 2004, there will be a greater clarity so that mutual needs and responsibilities are recognised and built into the programme at an early stage of planning.

The witness, analysis and evaluation by a staff member as the project unfolded, could be a monitoring contribution of significance, both currently and in the future.

A relaxed and even laid-back attitude by the leadership seemed to be the best way of operating, especially when there were difficulties which arose regularly from a variety of sources. There were a number of times when people did not deliver on their assurances and some expectations were not always fulfilled. It seemed important not to take things on, head to head, but rather to expect that problems would be overcome because of the trust that was shared. Hence, on a daily basis, the project moved on without being daunted by the regular appearance of flaws and cracks. They became part of the 'feast of learning', a term coined on the second day. This was applied when, occasionally, things happened which we would have preferred otherwise. The notion of flowing with the river, rather than fighting against it, normally produced effective resolutions without grievance.

The success of the third project meant that any further projects would require far greater organisation and personnel. Geoffrey had made it clear two years earlier that the project would need to operate so that it could be entrusted to a larger organisation which had the resources to take it forward on an international scale. In the next three months that was to come about.

5

An Act of Faith
The Entrustment

Less than three months later, on 30 September 2003, Geoffrey Whitfield and David Bedford, as an act of faith, entrusted the project to the British Council and the University of Brighton. In a little over three years, they had created a successful working project which could have international ramifications. The two of them had set out to create a project which could be handed on to an international body to develop throughout Israel and Palestine, and extend throughout the world. After the conclusion of the third project, they began to activate the original principle of entrusting the project to others, and consulted with a number of highly regarded international organisations to see how best this could be achieved. It was clear to them that the British Council and the University of Brighton could be among the key players in its future. What followed was a series of rapid developments which would bring about the essential strategic changes to its structure, as well as provision for tactical alterations.

In the three and a half years, what became the World Sports Peace Project had functioned basically as a non-governmental organisation, with the minimum of structure and personnel, and the maximum number of volunteers. Demonstrably, it was remarkably effective, but it would need to change if the future work was to be done by accountable bodies, with their own structures and rules of governance. Indeed, while there was the luxury of freedom to operate according to the united wisdom of the

126

participants on the Working Group, this might not be the case if formal organisations were to become involved. Officialdom required less unorthodoxy and more controls, as distinct from 'being led by the Spirit'. Fortunately, those who had joined the Working Group were already established and proven professionals. However, as the British Council became increasingly involved, it was inevitable that their ways of working were sometimes more demanding and less flexible than had previously been the case. Equally the University of Brighton's participation, which eventually involved increasing time and invisible expense, meant that they too were not free spirits. In the time between the third project and the 'act of faith', these issues would surface.

Yet the great strength of the project was in precisely that latitude which meant that there was a range of tolerance, as an innovative scheme took its own individual shape. It was not accountable except to the sense of professionalism that already profoundly existed in the Working Group. Mistakes were tolerated to provide the 'feast of learning', rather than an exactitude of individual behaviour. Thus any failure to deliver from time to time could be tolerated, with educational and healing space available for re-consideration and re-commitment. Authoritarian stances were foreign, and out of the spirit of the project.

Perhaps two differences related to issues of direct speech and of partnership. It had been the early culture that individuals had the confidence to speak directly to each other and have an exchange of views and differences without a go-between. If there was a difference, those concerned would handle it openly, rather than find someone else to deal with the issue. That meant that there was always person-to-person openness, without anyone having to field second-hand complaints of difficulty because of someone's fear of direct speech with a colleague. Equally, there was a sense of 'come let us reason together' rather than feeling that anyone had the authoritarian right to dictate to another or to make demands. That capacity to disagree without offence and to seek for the bigger picture meant a confidence within the founders. Issues of power, authority and control did not arise. No one ever reckoned to dictate to another, because colleagueship was of the essence. This was an exceptional rarity, but there was the unspoken understanding that the project was far bigger than any individual member.

Inevitably, there were differences in relating to indigenous non-Europeans who lived and worked in the Middle East. It was accepted that Arabs and Jews were rarely educated in the British system, but that they had their own valuable culture. It was rich, but not always easy, to work in a partnership where people had different standards and backgrounds. It would be inevitable that in a team, not everyone would understand leadership in terms of service and that the greatest leader needed to be the greatest servant. But the essence was to seek to behave in a way that was dignified, open, enlightened and harmonious in the attempt to bring out the best in each other by the exercise of insight, reason and patience.

These kinds of differences became more important in the summer months of transition. Geoffrey and David had made it clear from the outset that they would reckon to find others to take the project forward if a track record of success was made evident. This was repeated clearly in a number of ways and it was common parlance that the Group was working for its own redundancy. In anticipation of this, Geoffrey circulated papers on the philosophy, codes of practice, and the practicalities of future working partnerships, for the benefit of everyone involved.

WSPP Philosophy and Codes of Practice

WSPP has a Philosophy of Conflict Prevention through inter-community sport and social education.

WSPP is a UK voluntary organisation that initiates relation-ships with others in order to conduct annual Football/Conflict Prevention projects among children in Israel and Palestine, with a view to their wider extension in other communities and beyond the Middle East.

WSPP has a positive attitude in terms of how we conduct ourselves with dignity at all times in relation to mistakes, errors, follies, misunderstandings, differences, and disagreements.

WSPP seeks to be a catalyst for all that is constructive in relationships, whether personal, communal, national or interna-tional.

WSPP is less interested in blame and justifications, but is more interested in learning from human error and taking things forward to discover fresh pathways of progress.

WSPP stands for a way of finding pragmatic ways to relate to others who reflect a wholesome philosophy.

WSPP mirrors what we are by what we say and do; what we do not say and do not do.

WSPP endeavours to conduct business with integrity and grace, refraining from non-negotiable positions.

WSPP has a constant learning curve in order to work with those who are different and those who differ but are of good standing.

WSPP takes a positive and proactive view of linking formally with other organisations to discover ways of proceeding, whether in terms of alliance, partnership or association. At present, informal, exploratory conversations are taking place with the British Council, the University of Brighton, the Next Century Foundation, Care International and Save the Children Fund.

WSPP is flexible and is committed to taking responsible risks.

WSPP and practicalities of working with others

After three successful annual projects, the structure of WSPP needs to develop in order to adapt to the developments which will grow in the next three years from 2004–2006. This will involve exploring the potential for interdependently working with others, either in partnership, association or alliance. Among the key elements will be an Executive Director or equivalent, coaching teams from the UK, children, leadership and resources from Arab and Jewish communities, funding and equipment.

There will need to be at least two separate structures in order to deal with the project in Israel and the project in Bethlehem. The work in Bethlehem will not involve the British Embassy and the British Council in Tel Aviv but rather the Consulate General in Jerusalem and the British Council in East Jerusalem. This will necessitate the creation of two very separate structures.

The WSPP has the strengths of being a voluntary organisation where no one is paid by WSPP for their services. Each individual who participates has so far been financed from their own resources, whether their employment or their pension.

As an NGO, WSPP has the flexibility to work in ways that

129

might be difficult for a statutory organisation and this provides a strong independent side to complement any future structured alliance/partnership/association.

WSPP recognises the strength of having an alliance, partnership or association with formal structures which has access to resources of administration, finance and personnel as well as having public acceptance because of its status.

WSPP has the resources and expertise of the two co-founders which are available on a continuing basis, but any partnerships, alliances or associations must reckon on creating their own resources and expertise so that their availability is no longer necessary.

The knowledge of the people and the situations in Israel, Palestine and the UK, gathered by the WSPP over the years, is considerable, even unique, and can be made available to any alliances/partners/associates which might strengthen existing relationships and develop new ones.

WSPP will need to understand the complexities of other organisations such as the British Council which have different responsibilities, terms of reference and procedures of public accountability.

Interaction with the University of Brighton and the British Council

As the changes were being considered, there was haste, indeed, even an appetite, on the part of others, to take on such a successful and noteworthy project that had become widely respected.

The entrustment of the project to the British Council and the University of Brighton took place very quickly. Soon after the return to the UK in July there were a number of exchanges, particularly with the British Council and the different boundaries for the two became more apparent. Certain details were less essential to the Working Group, but nonetheless important for future co-operation and teamwork and these required face-to-face discussions in unhurried time. Time was not of the essence because the principle of transferring responsibilities in Israel to the British Council had already been discussed. Changes in the structure were to happen decently and in good order, and this was clearly apparent in correspondence between Geoffrey and Kevin Lewis throughout the month of July.

By the end of July it seemed clear from the exchange of correspondence that the British Council was happy to work in the UK with the University of Brighton, as it too had a formal infrastructure. This was compatible with the views of Geoffrey and David, as they had frequently and openly suggested this on a number of occasions. By the end of the month, there seemed to be a good mutual understanding of what needed to be done for the future development of the project, as World Sports Peace Project decreased and the input by the British Council and the University of Brighton increased. The options covered a number of rich alternatives, but it was essential that the main participants had the opportunity for having time together to consider them all.

On August 13, there was a meeting between Geoffrey, David, John and Gary at the offices of the Flora London Marathon and the future was even more clearly outlined. As a result, Geoffrey communicated the following information to Kevin Lewis.

"In the light of the success of the three projects in the Galilee region in the last three Summers, it is clear that there is the opportunity to expand in a way that is significant for the future. For this to be accomplished it seems right to us to suggest the following ideas:

1. The British Council in Israel could inherit the mantle in all aspects of our work hitherto. This could cover matters, first in terms of personnel and resources to administer the projects, secondly communities with their facilities, leaders and children, and thirdly finance, logistics and equipment.

2. In the UK, we have agreed to explore the idea of the Chelsea School of Physical Education of the University of Brighton becoming the co-ordinating agency in terms of recruitment of teams of coaches, their selection, education and training. It would also need to ensure that the ratio of available coaches was commensurate with the proposed number of children and venues.

3. The WSPP would be available in an advisory capacity for consultation when required.

4. The British Council in Israel and the UK could nominate a successor to Geoffrey to co-ordinate the work.

5. In order to begin to explore the possibilities outlined above, it would be helpful if there could be some exchange of ideas between yourself and the WSPP via Geoffrey fairly soon. These would be copied to the other three members of the core group for their feedback and contributions. Then in September we could have some clarity about the way ahead to organise these changes smoothly and effectively.

6. One special and particular concern is the outstanding commitment we in the WSPP have in terms of a two/three day project with the community in Beit Sahour in Bethlehem. Assuming that the security situation is resolved by summer, 2004, there could be some discussions about how this might be organised. We are very sensitive to the issue of separate responsibilities within the British Council and British Embassy, but feel they could be resolved fairly simply, as proposed in 2002.

7. We would hope that it will be possible for there to be a meeting in the UK between you and ourselves on Wednesday, September 17, for us to talk in detail about the foregoing. If we all feel that this is a progressive way forward, we could discuss the timetable for a changeover of responsibilities without difficulty."

At the time, there was no response to this communication and, therefore, it was expected that the points would have been taken on board.

There were other essential matters to be considered. The first was that despite the previous experience that existed in the team already, clearly it had not been sufficiently expert to produce a satisfactory Conflict Prevention component in terms of Social Education. Further expertise was essential and Geoffrey had made explorations with the Bradford University of Peace Studies Department for their possible involvement in the future. Secondly, the involvement of the film crew from Southampton Institute of Higher Education had provided an essential ingredient in publicity and record keeping, and their future involvement needed serious consideration. Thirdly, there remained the commitment to the Rapprochement Centre in Bethlehem, which needed to be kept to the forefront.

It was known that any fulfilment of these intentions of the WSPP would mean considerable commitment by any major player in the future, whether it was Save the Children or Olympic Aid, as originally considered, or now, the British Council and the

University of Brighton. Any major organisation should be allowed to develop the project in their way, as they would have responsibility for it in the foreseeable future. The time was at hand for World Sports Peace Project to remove itself from the scene.

Geoffrey maintained contact with David, Kevin, John and Gary, covering issues as they developed. In summary, he wrote that they could meet on September 17 in Brighton to take discussions another significant step forward, bearing in mind the following considerations:

When Geoffrey and David planned the operation in 2000, it was with a view to handing over the project, if successful, to another organisation or institution or NGO. Their intention was that such a body would be in a position to develop the project and to extend it on an international scale beyond the Middle East, which is where they planned to begin. Thus any future partners would need to understand the philosophy of the project as being beyond sport, involving wider issues, and to have the vision and resources for any development.

Having now reached the point where we have invited the British Council in Israel to take responsibility for the project in that country and similarly invited the University of Brighton to co-ordinate the project in the UK, we now need to move on to discuss the details. Although we have not formally taken this further, it is hoped that the meeting on the 17th will take serious steps in that direction. Equally, although there has been no formal response from the University, it is hoped that this can also eventually be taken forward.

We need to be conscious that the British Council in Israel is limited to that country and cannot be involved elsewhere. Similarly, the University of Brighton has many resources and skills available, but they do not claim to be experts in peace studies. Thus it is necessary to be clear that it is not reasonable to expect them to take over the project without further careful consideration and the possible inclusion of others.

The meeting between Geoffrey, David, Kevin, John and Gary took place on September 17 in a very convivial atmosphere. In summary the British Council offered either to take responsibility for the organisation of the project development in Israel, including taking the lead in fund-raising and relating to one major body in the UK (i.e. the University of Brighton), or to have a partnership with the University of Brighton and work out separate responsibilities. With either of these two options, they would need to be properly documented and presented to the Working Group before final approval could be agreed. The British Council also hoped that financial help could still be forthcoming from the Flora London Marathon.

A number of important and significant matters were also raised in relation to details mentioned above, pending further consideration and discussion to take place on September 30 at the next WSPP meeting in London. These had been included in the agenda and were specified as follows:

➤ The place and inclusion of expert 'Peace Studies' input, hopefully from Bradford University;
➤ The place and inclusion of Southampton Institute of Higher Education and their strategic, long-term connections with the media and Southampton FC;
➤ The place and inclusion of World Vision, Jerusalem, in relation to the project in Bethlehem;
➤ The position of the WSPP Executive Director and the future replacement for his work.

It was expected that further discussion would take place at that WSPP meeting on Tuesday, September 30. No final decision date was arranged, but the meeting was felt by everyone as very positive so far. The meeting ended with it being mentioned that Kevin would be going to the University in Eastbourne the next day to see the sports facilities and to meet the staff.

The following afternoon, John Sugden sent an email to Geoffrey. There had been a meeting with Kevin and colleagues at the Chelsea School that morning who had agreed a partnership arrangement between the University of Brighton (UoB) and the British Council (BC), although none of this had been introduced or discussed the previous evening in Brighton when they had met formally:

➤ This (partnership between the University and the British

134

Council) will immediately and effectively take over the running of the Galilee project for the foreseeable future.
➤ The key strategic decisions will be made by the BC in consultation with the UoB via John Sugden.
➤ The UoB will have specific responsibility for UK volunteers.
➤ The BC Israel will have executive authority.
➤ As such, the overview function of WSPP with regard to this particular project will cease to exist. The Galilee project will be outside its executive authority.

Report of the final meeting, 30 September 2003

Geoffrey indicated that the task of the meeting was to move ahead and to be creative.

The video of the project which had been produced by the Southampton Institute of Higher Education was shown and well received by everyone.

David Bedford then addressed the major item which was the future of the projects. The WSPP had created, in three years, what had been blessed and become a real achievement in Israel between the Arab and Jewish communities. Few projects had got as far as this. It was the start of the future, and the meeting had to decide where to go from here as it needed a change of direction, with greater input to take it forward. It was a very successful project, and ripe to be handed on to another structure. Good relationships had been constructed with the British Council in Israel and the University of Brighton in the UK. They would inherit a successful project, which we could leave to them to develop. The UoB and BC would be asked to report back to WSPP to provide information, and for advice or support.

Geoffrey supported the views of David, although with some serious reservations about matters still outstanding which needed to be addressed. These included the crucial nature of ongoing consultation with those involved, and the avoidance of imposition which could otherwise poison any chance of creative relationships. His role, which from the beginning had been an exploratory one, brought information for colleagues to discuss before decisions were made and this spirit should be continued. The British Council had shown increasing interest following early

135

contact by Geoffrey. From the Autumn of 2001, a warm colleague-ship had blossomed, subsequent to the success of the first project that year, and a unity of purpose was created, based on mutual trust and vision.

The Conflict Prevention side of the project, which was the most important, had also been the most difficult. Therefore the project would need to seek the assistance of those who were experts in that field, because clearly the project was not yet sufficiently effective or it would have been more successful. The Bradford University Peace Studies Department had been approached, as they had a Chair of Conflict Prevention with a specialist on the Middle East, and were open to further discussions.

Geoffrey also raised the matter of commitment to the Rapprochement Centre in Beit Sahour, Bethlehem and the advantage of continued liaison with World Vision, which had responsibility for both Israel and the West Bank, unlike the British Council and the British Embassy in Tel Aviv who were not allowed to cover the two areas.

Jim Doyle of Southampton Institute of Higher Education said he would be glad to have the University of Brighton in the driving seat and that the Institute would still like to be involved. He thought that the project had huge potential for Conflict Prevention as well as research and funding.

John Sugden said he had had experience and responsibilities in peace work in Northern Ireland in the 1980s and did not need lessons regarding Conflict Prevention in the Middle East. In relation to Galilee, he saw the need for control and accountability. He would listen to wise counsel from outside, but there was no place for other organisations apart from the BC. The UoB could handle the organisational work in the UK.

Gary Stidder said that he saw the video as marking the end of the present project, with WSPP handing on to the University of Brighton and the British Council. Carl Dearing of Southampton supported the handing on to the BC and UoB. He saw the weakness so far in relation to Conflict Prevention and felt that there was a need for outside assistance, for example, philosophy students, and hoped that the manual being prepared by UoB, in relation to team-building, would help.

David pointed out that the discussions held by Geoffrey with other parties had been right and had created no conflict in so doing. The way ahead was to hand on the Israel side of the project to the British Council in Tel Aviv. When Geoffrey raised the obligation WSPP had to Bethlehem, John and Gary said they felt it morally right to seek to fulfil that responsibility.

David proposed a statement of intent to the University of Brighton and the British Council, which would include the matter of Bethlehem, and a request for a report and consultation with WSPP on progress and developments. Geoffrey and David could draft such a statement and consult the group for comments before it was sent. It would include:

> The expressed desire for it to be handed on, as an "Act of Faith", to the British Council and the University who were in a position to see to its extension and success;
> the understanding that they had access to resources of personnel and funding;
> they should bear in mind the existing commitment to Bethlehem;
> the request for reporting back to WSPP where they can follow progress and be supportive where appropriate.

Geoffrey asked about the formal structures within the University and the British Council and the matter of formal acknowledgements, documentation and the proper channels within their structures. It was essential that what was being discussed was not purely an arrangement between individuals, so that the project might collapse with the demise of any one person. John Sugden assured the meeting that such arrangements would be official and said he would brief both the University Vice-Chancellor and the Head of Chelsea School of Physical Education.

Geoffrey supported the change of name for the future projects as it would not be appropriate for the new structure to use WSPP any longer in relation to this development. Geoffrey agreed that he and David would communicate with a range of people and organisations to acquaint them with the changes and the new arrangements, particularly the new BC/UoB structure which would not use the WSPP title, but create another suitable alternative.

Other matters concerned the successes of Galilee July 2003, especially the liaison with the Israel Embassy. The learning points were also noted, especially relations with the hotel management. In terms of our reputation being damaged, misunderstood or misrepresented it was important to note recurring issues, although they would no longer be of concern to WSPP: these were connected to security and issues of racism which would be of concern to the British Council and the Football Association.

The meeting ended with David Bedford expressing warm and generous appreciation for the input of Geoffrey during the life-time of the project, saying that without his initiatives the project would never have happened. There was no date fixed for a 'next meeting' as the future structure was not the remit of the WSPP. The two co-founders remained as the sole principals of the World Sports Peace Project.

A formal notice in November, from Geoffrey and David as co-founders, was sent to political and other official bodies and agencies, including the media.

Exciting Developments in the World Sports Peace Project

It is with a great sense of accomplishment that we look back over the last three years and see the success of our annual Football/Conflict Prevention projects in Galilee between Jewish and Arab youngsters and their communities. We have appreciated the help of many people both in the UK and Israel and now, with a proven track record, it is appropriate to move ahead with fresh organisational structures.

The British Council in Israel and the Chelsea School of Physical Education of the University of Brighton have especially given impressive commitment to our projects. As we contemplate the future, we are glad that they have shown great eagerness to continue with the project in their own ways and, as an act of faith, we are able to entrust the future project to them. We have been assured that it will become embedded into the formal structures of both organisations, with a fresh title. We anticipate that it will be seen primarily as a Conflict Prevention project that uses football to carry this through. To achieve this, we commend the continuing interaction with organisations such as Givat Haviva in Israel and the exploratory discussions with others involved in peace work in the UK, especially the Peace Studies Department of the University of Bradford.

We also encourage the British Council and the University of Brighton to continue to find fresh, innovative ways of maintaining consultative interactions with others in both countries. Hopefully it will be developed successfully and prove to be of growing influence and become a model for other communities and countries.

The World Sports Peace Project will value being kept informed and updated with developments on a regular and systematic basis.

Co-founders: GEOFFREY WHITFIELD AND DAVID BEDFORD

※

Postscript

It was gratifying to have updates from John Sugden over the next six months. In November, he confirmed that the project was in 'safe and institutionally secure hands'. He also referred to developments with the British Council in Israel and the organisation of a meeting with the three partner institutions of St Mary's College, Twickenham, Brunel University and Southampton Institute of Higher Education.

This was followed by further correspondence in December when he confirmed more progress:

1. The project would now be called 'Football 4 Peace' and they wished to use part of the WSPP logo of the dove and olive branch.
2. There was to be a structured programme from 28 March – 1 April 2004, for municipal community sports leaders and coaches from Israel who would work with the UK coaches, in preparation for the summer project.
3. They had produced the training manual which, presumably, referred to the Conflict Prevention side of the projects, although this had yet to be fully accomplished.
4. From 1–11 July 2004, there would be 700 children from 14 communities, including a significant contingent of girls. This would be serviced by 28 UK coaches and seven leaders. It was also intended to include a film crew from Southampton Institute of Higher Education, but this was not carried through.

The "Act of Faith" was nonetheless moving ahead in gratifying ways. On 31 March 2004, Geoffrey was invited to Eastbourne for a dinner, where over 60 staff from Israel and the UK had been working for four days. He was invited to speak, and he said how utterly moving it was for him to be there, and to see the incredible way the project was being taken forward. He said he would never forget that evening as he looked around that mass of warmth and firm intent. One of the first partners in the original project in 2001, Auni Edris, the sports director of Ibillin, came forward and made a delightful and much appreciated presentation to him and to John Sugden.

The following evening there was another meeting, this time at Arsenal FC at Highbury. The coaches had spent the final day there, and Geoffrey was there again for a special reason which he had discussed with John Sugden. Throughout the four years, the project had received great commendations, and it was usually directed at Geoffrey Whitfield, as Executive Director of the project. He was all too aware that none of it would have been possible without the 'invisible man', David Bedford. Because Geoffrey knew David would also be invited to Highbury, he contacted Raji Srouji, the sports director of Nazareth, and arranged for him to bring a presentation plate from Nazareth Municipality. When Geoffrey was invited to address the meeting, he used the occasion to address the subject of David's partnership, and spoke of his immense input over the years. He asked David to come forward from the back of the room, and for Raji Srouji, to come and make the presentation. David came to the front to receive the gift, and as he did so, the whole room stood and applauded him at length. It was an unforgettable occasion.

Recognition

But even more was to come. In October 2004, the World Sports Peace Project, and all who had been involved in it, was honoured when Geoffrey received the MBE from Her Majesty the Queen at Buckingham Palace. When she asked him about how he became involved in the project, he avoided her question and briefly outlined the project itself. As he was speaking, her face changed into a warm, beaming smile as, in only a few seconds, she recognised the significance of the undertaking. She said to him: "This could make such a difference."

A further momentous celebration took place on 28 July 2005, as David Bedford was made an Honorary Doctor of Science by the University of Brighton on its Graduation Day for his achievements in, and service to, sport, in which his part as co-founder of the World Sports Peace Project was also publicly recognised.

6

A Model for the Church, Sport and Conflict Prevention

The story of this project might be said to begin with: "There's a football supporter here who has three footballs and some shorts." It is similar to: "There's a lad here with five loaves and two fishes", which was the beginning of one of the miracle stories, known as the 'Feeding of the Five Thousand'. But the footballs and shorts were for a youth club near Nazareth and pretty soon, Jew and Arab youngsters were playing football in mixed teams while, elsewhere, there was bombing and violence, including youngsters who were throwing stones and getting hurt and killed. The project was just a modern day miracle.

The World Sports Peace Project (WSPP) began innocently enough as a basic enterprise, silently based on religious attitudes and actions, and ended up demonstrating for some, the relevance of Christianity as a contribution to the work of both Terrorism Prevention and Conflict Resolution. The definition of words such as terrorism, violence and conflict, although important elsewhere, did not seem crucial when one was dealing with divided communities alienated by fear. Moreover, although the project was inspired by the logical consequence of Christian belief and practice, it did not set out to make Christians from other beliefs. It was true that there was a desire to be dynamically involved in the implications of peace on earth and goodwill to all people. However, the project never sounded off about its origins, and simply developed into a project which involved believers in Christianity, Islam and Judaism, to say nothing about those who held no such convictions. There were no outward religious symbols, no faith statements and no demands for any. It was, outwardly, a simple enterprise which was intended to lead to the prevention and resolution of violence because those who participated had to work together as a team and leave behind animosities, prejudices and fears, if they were to succeed. Ultimately this was intended to make a significant contribution towards peace and hope, at a time when, elsewhere, there was violence and terror. This claim could be made by every person who took part, whether religious or otherwise. It drew people together without needing to make reference to personal creeds or affiliations. It was a pinnacle for the sublime nature of humanity. It was a project, open to all, begun by a few Christians because they saw it as the right thing for them to do, rather than as an invitation for people to come and be a part of a Christian project.

The project had no need for obvious labels for the purposes of religious identification because its driving force was the logical consequence of a belief in peace, whatever the origin of that faith. It was an unspoken statement about God and His love for all people, and His will for them to be a community of love instead of being in a state of alienation from each other.[4] In essence the project was about reconciliation and offered hope, which blossomed into confidence. It was possible for it to be considered one small step in the Pleroma[5] which is a religious word meaning the ultimate goal for the whole of humanity. It is important now to bring to the fore some of the concepts which, although non-intrusive, were for some, pulsating at the heart of the project.[6]

This final chapter identifies a number of emerging, religious themes. It represents only one Christian point of view, and others can offer their own interpretations. This does not commence with a series of propositions and then trace how they were implemented, nor does it follow a conventional system of presenting theology. Instead it uncovers a series of themes which imperceptibly surfaced, as a growing company of people emerged to put ideas into practice, and then strangely discovered stepping stones only after they had walked on them. Although the stones had been at the ground of the project all the time, this only became apparent with hindsight and after much reflection. This process was less to do with looking back at the project to discover the theological milestones that had been followed; rather it was to do with recognising there had been a journey which unconsciously choreographed spiritual values and insights, and resulted in the explosion of positive ideas. This led to an expedition of faith, whereby sometimes there were signposts and sometimes not, but the journey was still sustained. It probably came close to what a German scholar named Karl Barth called "a human response to revelation".[7] Gradually the insights became increasingly clear, and influenced behaviour as well as the standards and vision of the project whereby its goal was preserved as bigger than sport, and more to do with hidden values of all authentic religion.

The influences? The discovery of revelation?

Some influences may be considered part of a 'top-down' process of energy and action. Thus some people behave in a certain way because they are ordered or taught to do so, either by command or written orders. For other people it is much less obvious, and only in becoming involved in an activity can they, with hindsight, look back and see that they have been activated by a source, which only afterwards became clear. This might be considered a 'bottom-up' activity or process, and this is what seemed to characterise the whole project. The hand of God became more clearly noticeable for some as the project got underway, rather than showing itself as a preconceived set of instructions to be followed. However, with hindsight, there were simple biblical principles in operation which stemmed, for example, from St John's Gospel where Jesus spoke of the vine and the branches, and the natural movement of creative life passing invisibly and slowly from the roots of the vine to the branches to produce the visible grape harvest.[8]

One may ask the question: Why was such a project in Israel never activated before? Indeed, there may possibly have been similar operations elsewhere. Why was it that, when the proposition was put to certain people, so many said: 'Of course'? It seemed so obvious to suggest that people who came from backgrounds of alienation could be brought together to do something enriching and creative with each other. It seemed even more obvious and simple that, if they worked together as a team, instead of retaining their hostile positions, they could success-fully achieve a common goal and come out afterwards feeling quite differently about each other. The symbolic nature of such simplicity through teamwork made it even more evident that this could be replicated anywhere in similar circumstances. Since it commenced in 2000, similar initiatives have appeared in parts of Israel and elsewhere, involving people who had little contact with each other when this project first started.

In writing about peace processes between divided countries, the writer and broadcaster, Oliver McTernan wrote:

A peace process that fails to take time to engage local communi-ties and to build bridges both within and between them, religious and secular, is unlikely to survive the tensions festering below the surface of either community . . . The total collapse of the peace process in Israel/Palestine is hardly surprising, as I met no one at a community level on either side who felt in any way a part of the Oslo and Camp David meetings. There is a clear and urgent need to strengthen the local peace-building capacity at a street level in parallel with the initiation of political talks at the top leadership level.[9]

Those who initiated the WSPP did so as a natural movement rather than as part of a thought through strategy. Somewhere in this there could be found the motivating experience of what some call the Holy Spirit, who not only guides humanity into ways of living and behaving, but opens their eyes, enabling them to see possibilities for something connected to the peace of God. In relation to this particular project, it was deduced later that the project had come from some blend of internal discernment, moulded into shape by the Spirit of God, and was bigger than human initiative alone. This gave the assurance that the project was larger than reason alone, and that not only could human insights be acted on, but vision provided and resilience supported in grounded ways of endurance. This could be called the active reinforcement of the Paraclete, another word for the One who, invisibly, stands shoulder to shoulder, to enable the person under pressure to persevere.[10] This action can now, with hindsight, be called practical faith by some or 'Applied Theology' by others.

The project seemed gradually to pulsate in the first place to the group of Christian leaders in Israel and the UK, and later surfaced in a number of ways as peacemaking, reconciliation, hope and outright pleasure. It did not start out with an obvious, stated religious premise on which it was built. However, this was easier to see at the conclusion in 2003 rather than at its commencement in 2000. Instead of seeking to impose religious principles from the top, theology was noticed or revealed as the project emerged and developed. It would have been understandable if there had been some clear inspirational sense of Christian calling, with all the reassurance that such an experience can provide. With hindsight it could be recognised that some of the religious background was interwoven with issues of suffering and fear, as well as hatred and revenge. Only looking back could it be seen that the influence of people such as Martin Luther King Jnr.,[11] already integrated by Geoffrey and others, had become an invisible part of the pattern emerging from the warp and woof of the tapestry being created.

At the end, there was a sense of a different metaphor, that of having created a trail through a jungle, although, paradoxically, throughout the journey there was the intention that something tangible and specific would come to view. As it turned out, the result, considering the context, verged on the miraculous. It was more a case of 'Stand still and see the salvation of the Lord',[12] rather than imposing a particular belief system on a different culture and community. In another context it could be considered as an Epiphany that very slowly unfolded in their growing awareness over time. It showed its face in 2000, for example, with a man from Brighton named Alan Pook offering three footballs for a youth club in Galilee. With hindsight he can be seen as the modern day equivalent of someone saying: "There's a lad here with five loaves and two fishes."[13] It is hopefully not too arrogant to consider the project was part of the process of responding to divine revelation.

Mystery and immanence

The WSPP process, therefore, does not seem to have come from a clear set of instructions or leading. It came about as the self-evident thing to do, and only later was it possible to reflect on the source of the drive or initiative. There seemed to be an influence outside of oneself, almost an immanence, beyond the words which might adequately explain the experience. It was too coincidental for the project to be only a set of coincidences! That drive, while undramatic, had to come from the initiative of the Holy Spirit within the human catalysts of the project, just like many 'stimulus-response' activities. If so, what was in the understanding of those who started the project, so that what they did was part of a natural progression? What was the unknown, but integrated mindset that appeared to provoke an automatic response to a given situation, rather than a conscious working of the intellect, almost like programming by a computer, or the shoots appearing on a branch after the darkness of the winter? Moreover, not to have followed that instinctive response to the stimulus would have been almost impossible for those concerned. Surely this was an experience of what used to be called 'the numinous', or the idea of the holy, as originally stated a century ago by Rudolph Otto. It could be the acknowledgement and outworking of the words of a prophet, who spoke of the Lord putting his law in the minds and hearts of his people.[14]

Is it possible that, if someone professes to follow Christ or some other belief system, there is a 'conditioning' and, although the person operates by judgement and choice and not as an automaton, he or she appears to be as close to instinct as one can contemplate? Is it because there is significance in the notion that, if they have a relationship with Christ or Allah or God as they experience and understand Him, then they have an internal model for their behaviour? While there are many who will avow that truth, and yet behave very differently to others with similar convictions, there is a modelling that flows from the divine–human relationship.

Hence, was it not natural that, if one heard someone in Ibillin saying in 1994: "We have no books and we need a library for the children", one automatic response could be: "Here, have some of mine"? And so a village library came into being. Perhaps the response was based on 'human care and concern' for some people, but for others it may have been something additional, from a source of the Spirit, that had been experienced, assimilated and integrated, invisible but ready also for an outward flow. At this point we are perhaps touching the area of mystery, rather than any scientific rationale for 'instinct', and this necessitates trying to locate the tangible elements within the mystery.

Motivation and behaviour is made up of more than insight, intelligence or relevant external assistance. These internal receptors which activate positive responses are like catalysts for ignition, or germinating seeds. They are not only religious. These processes, however defined, mean that individuals can be tuned into certain inputs which bring about immediate responses, such as sport, or sex, music, fear, comfort or violence, to name but a few. Many responses are learned, so what is the distinctive stimulus for the flow of Christian service? What is the external catalyst for the human catalyst? Some would call that primary source the Holy Spirit, but are there other additional factors for inclusion and consideration? Where is the place for modelling, whether Jesus Christ, a saint, a friend or a family member? Thus, what a person may do, could be what was first demonstrated by another, so that it was copied or assimilated, or both, and unconsciously passed on to be repeated.

There have to be other factors, such as concepts, that are integrated and acted out in a range of situations. When a person has integrated the Lord's Prayer for example, they may develop an impulse to act upon the words, 'Your will be done on earth'.[15] Or one may follow the prayer of St Francis and find oneself, without realising it at that precise moment, moving to act out, 'Make me a channel of your peace'. The integration of certain passages of scripture may also act as the starting point for an individual who seeks to be a social reformer, or an agent of social change. Equally, the individual may be able to set aside their own need for wealth, in order to bring about some change in the conditions of people. Others may take a wider view of influence, and seek to move to pivotal places, in order to bring about changes in circumstances elsewhere. Christian Socialism and other forms of political and social reform, like those of William Wilberforce and his efforts for slave trade reform, had their roots in that tradition.

More than humanism

In relation to this special project, there were religious principles functioning throughout which, although well-known by some, were not publicly placed at its forefront. The project was considered to be based upon more than humanism by the originators, who had different views of the world and humanity which were basically theological, and led to a sequence of beliefs. Probably one of the prime, invisible, unspoken factors concerned the sacredness of humanity – that no one is superior or inferior to the other in ultimate terms, and all have equal inalienable and infinite dignity. It infers that no one is more or less sacred than the other because all are made by God, with purposes that are beyond the material and the political. This view was not better or worse than any of the views of the other partners, nor were these opinions discussed in any depth, but it did mean that motivations were different. They were part of their internal philosophy and belief systems, and accounted for their personal drive and vision. With hindsight it was recognised that some of the team had a sense of 'ultimate accountability'[16] to God. This was not in terms of reward or punishment, rather they saw themselves as agents, or representatives, with a different scale of reference and different resources. Their drive was connected to their understanding of the will of God being worked out in terms of: 'Thy will be done on earth'. Others who joined in the project had views and opinions which had their own bases, and together they created a formidable team. No one was asked for a particular set of values, except those that the project stood for, which was conflict prevention through sport, involving a wide range of people with and without faith.

However, if it is true that Christianity is a transcendent form of humanism, insofar as it bridges the gap between the apex of human achievement and the ultimate of human need and aspiration, then in Christian action there is present a quality of unique and distinctive meaning which motivates the individual. Values of faith become essential and consciously crucial for the spirit of that person, and the enterprise in which he or she is involved.

Creation, humanity and its destiny

One fundamental principle, which remained unspoken at the time, was a particular view that the world was created by God.

This view was not shared by all the participants but led on to a range of opinions. They were not exhaustive, but they were pivotal in describing a privately held approach to this particular peace project. It meant that the Creation stories of the book of Genesis indicated that the world belonged to God, and not to any earthly power. It did not ultimately belong to any one race, and all of humanity was called to continue the beautiful process of Creation, as co-creators with God.

The message of the Creation stories could be applied to certain attitudes to land, especially in the disputed territory of Israel and Palestine, more in terms of stewardship of resources, and less in terms of exploitation of those resources and the people of the land. It also implies that anyone involved in an undertaking, from this theological perspective, would need to work with a global scale of reference, and not otherwise. This could have become a volatile subject of disagreement had it been aired. One Judaic interpretation was apparently simple for some and developed further; the land was given to the Jews by this Creator God as they understood Him, for their exclusive use as His chosen people and was not to be divided or shared. Others interpret the same sources differently and with vigour. The issue of the land is a fraught one for both Israeli Arabs and Jews and would become volatile in any discussions between the two Semitic peoples. However, the practical theology of a project, such as the one that is the focus here, provided a totally different context for people to meet and discuss opportunities for mutual involvement, as distinct from those who strongly represented different interests. It did serve to indicate that, for the people of faith or without it, there could be places of respect and accord from which to commence discussions which could lead to some mutuality of mind, heart and spirit. These could create different mindsets of co-operative appreciation for those who might later need to discuss issues of greater moment.

In so many ways, the WSPP provided a commonality for new attitudes towards each other, as distinct from communities elsewhere that had not experienced the same opportunities for togetherness. It is now possible to envisage the far-reaching effects of cordiality, whereby significant and long-held differences could one day be discussed in a very different atmosphere because of the effects of the non-aligned experience offered by

WSPP. Any change in attitude by the Israeli and Arab hierarchies would be difficult to imagine at this stage in history, and any adjustment to that position might more likely be envisaged if it came from within the communities rather than from an external source. It was important to the project that it kept within the boundaries of what it could constructively accomplish in terms of relationships and working at the prevention of violence in all its forms.

It could be argued that the logo of the project, drawn from the story of Noah and the Flood,[17] conveyed the message of the global scope of the project. It consisted of a dove in flight with a piece of an olive twig in its beak, its body being spherically shaped, both as the globe of the world, and as a football. This could be understood as a symbol of wholeness and completion, influenced by the symbol of God's Spirit and intention of peace. Interestingly, it was first sketched, not by a Christian or a Jew but by a Moslem.

The Genesis stories state that the world belongs to God, and to be parochial and possessive is to be small-minded. The WSPP saw the need to have its strategy on the widest scale, so that it embraced the cosmos. Therefore the Christians who were involved in the project always tried to have the bigger picture of: 'Your will be done on earth'.[18] The view was taken that the land never did belong exclusively to Jews or Arabs, or people of any faith or none, but to God. That provided the ground, or strategy, for Christian theology because the 'owners' were understood to be stewards, and those who lived on it were called to be a light to the nations and not otherwise.

The Creation story gave a bigger picture to any enterprise, so that it could be seen as part of a larger framework, rather than something more limited. Humanity was commanded to be involved in the ongoing process of Creation.[19] There was a backcloth to any project, insofar as it was another piece of co-creation, as part of the overall drama of ongoing creation. Creation was not a once and for all act of God, but a process which involved the planet becoming a sphere which declared the glory of God by the way people lived in it, and with each other. To those who had this attitude, it gave a wider perspective to the situation, and offered hope in any presenting task to be undertaken. It was separate from the view of those faiths which hold different opinions about the Creation as an activity of God, for then they can have different ways of understanding the world and its resources. The planet Earth has significance for the Christian, in ultimate terms, which means there is a different quality of respect for its present use and ultimate intentions; not superior, but different.

One theological perspective in the project was a view of humanity that led to another sequence. Humanity was seen as good, having been made by God and in his image. Humanity was not seen originally as bad. The story of the creation of humanity, and the Garden of Eden, speak of the worth and dignity of humanity, and their relationships. Their destiny is to inherit the earth and to turn it into a blessed place, as befits a people of dignity. The consequence is that to be destructive of the Creation, and the humanity that God created, would be a denial of that dignity and their destiny. This is a very different view to that of the Arab and Jew in Israel and Palestine, to say nothing of the USA and the rest of the world. Interactive violence and hatred towards each other is destructive of any notion of behaving with dignity or treating the other with dignity.

One consequence was a current of hope running through the project that the ultimate destiny of those involved was to live in harmony. The mixture of the cultures involved, to say nothing of the mixture of personalities, provided the ingredients for energy which could be creative or otherwise. For the project, the theological significance of the sense of the destiny of the people and the land, even though very different to the indigenous Arab and Jewish cultures, gave a capacity for endurance and optimism. This provided the ground for being undeterred by difficulties and disappointments which emerged from time to time. It meant that there was always a permanent mindset of creative, practical optimism, whatever negative experience emerged. There was an infinite capacity to endure, when circumstances brought setbacks, whether locally, or in the bigger picture of wider events in the land.

Service, Community and Stewardship

The core attitudes and beliefs led to certain standards of behaviour in terms of leadership and association. Those who joined the partnership came from different cultures and mindsets, and this affected how leadership and team work were understood. There was one specific understanding of the theological nature of leadership which was understood by the project originators in terms of service and servanthood, rather than power and control.[20] Moreover, there was no need for extra payment because it was a Christian responsibility, but this idea was not always shared by those who were to become colleagues. However, those who came from the UK worked as volunteers and no one was paid for their participation in the project. This meant that no one could say that those involved were gaining financially from their involvement. Thus when people gathered around the table, and came as leaders within their own community, they brought their own working practices, methods of operating, and belief systems. Inevitably these would differ, both consciously and unconsciously, but the larger vision of the project was bigger than any personal, financial gain.

Perhaps one regular experience which arose was when accepted practice in many places was contrary to the expectations of others. One example was when people would ignore requests for information prior to a meeting so that everyone could be informed ahead of time but instead, matters would be raised at the table without warning. It was also practice for discussions to take place in private before a meeting, so that only those who had been participants were prepared for what was to come. Equally the 'laws' of group dynamics[21] were to be revealed in terms of the 'hidden leader', and 'pairing', 'in group and out group', all of which, elsewhere, were quite regular ways of operating. However, they were not always in the best interests of overall team building, and were sometimes used to create a position of strength or even opportunism. This did not mean that those who so behaved were better or worse than others, but that they were different in terms of partnership, as others were influenced by theological concepts which underlaid their ideas of practice and trust.

This also applied to the meaning and use of words and agreements, which would be made in one place and either not carried through, or simply denied. It became difficult in two particular ways, as one Arab colleague laughingly joked: "When an Arab or a Jew uses the word 'Yes' or 'No', they can have very different meanings!" The theology behind "Let your 'Yea' be 'Yea' and

153

your 'Nay' be 'Nay'",[22] was suddenly very appropriate. This could also be seen in the close relationships within extended families and those outside. The Europeans sometimes found it hard to appreciate the internal connections and loyalties which existed in both Arab and Jewish familial and social constructions. It is normal in some societies for some family members to be given automatic preference over others. This kind of value system affects many parts of the society, and reveals different understandings and uses of integrity. What the western mind dismisses as 'Nepotism' fails to understand the origins of eastern family and community loyalties which come from a different base. For example, when the Jews were first a minority tribe in Israel, they learned the essential nature of strong familial and societal connections. That solidarity gave them a security not to be put at risk.[23] The present concerns for strict cleanliness, and Sabbath observance, seem not only based on piety, but also on anxiety which possibly contributed then and now to the focus on scrupulous attention to many forms of Jewish religious life. The WSPP offered a different understanding of community life and cultural interaction. While the theologically minded turn to the way that Jesus referred to families as being under the fatherhood of God, and the brotherhood of man, there were current cultural differences in the process of relationships and decision making. These needed to be appreciated and understood so that there were not grounds for serious misunderstanding.

It was at the points of difference that the issues of commonality came to the fore. Here the strengths of the project were tested and it was important that they were seen as more enduring than the differences, whatever they were. It was essential to see the project in a wider context than whether or not the partners came from and shared the same mindsets. It was also essential for the practicalities of the project, as well as for modelling for other groups, that there was the capacity to absorb without offence the differences and practices of colleagues from different traditions, belief systems and cultures. With this particular multi-cultural and multi-faith enterprise there needed to be sufficient objectivity and belief in the basic concepts, not to be overtaken by differences of perception or behaviour. Instead differences were used as opportunities for further sensitivity, patience and appreciation of one another, as a continuous learning curve, rather than a ground for non-co-operation. This was especially noticeable in the first project in 2001 when the Jewish community in Misgav withdrew from the project for their own reasons. Although it had undermined confidence at first, the community was given an open door without recrimination the following year when they indicated they wished to be included in the future. This was evidence of applied theology in action, for the roots of the reconciliation attitude were theological. It was critical to create the mindset of moving ahead whenever difficulties emerged, rather than to become submerged in a culture of taking up time on blame and justification. It has to be admitted that, with both Eastern and Western colleagues, this was not always simple to accomplish!

Differences in religious practice and dialogue

These ways of operating were all adjacent to openly religious views. Nominally the Europeans, Israeli Arabs and Israeli Jews were seen to represent the three monotheistic faiths, when in actual fact it was not the case at all. Not all Europeans wished to be regarded as Christians, even if that is how they were perceived. Equally Israeli Arabs were likely to be Christians, as well as Moslems or Druze.[24] The range of belief and practice within Judaism in Israel is rarely possible to perceive and understand. However, some religious observances did come to the fore at the weekends as each religious group had its own 'day of rest'. There was no question of the Jewish Shabbat being used for the final tournament – everything had to be completed well before sundown to enable people to get home. This did not mean that those so committed were necessarily devout, but they responded quite naturally to the cultural system that was embedded in their nominal religious adherence.

While no one made any particular open claim to religious belief, nor referred to it, it was salutary that Christians, Moslems and Jews, whether Israeli or European, were involved in a hectic and committed project from the outset. Yet religious leaders never appeared as such, except on one occasion. A small group of Baptist ministers gave up their time, and came out of their way, to come to the final tournament in 2002. Their question was simple: "How many believers have you made?" For them it was an issue very close to proselytism, and they were confused and surprised that so much effort was going into an event which was more openly focused on social, political and cultural ends. The words of Christ: 'Your will be done on earth'[25] were conceded almost as an afterthought, and were not at the forefront in their thinking. They would have agreed about the need for justice and peace being the will of God, but would not have interpreted the words in the same way as the project members. Moreover, while it was apparent to the visitors about the need to make disciples, there seemed to be little afterwards except to make still more disciples, rather than to work for the Kingdom of God in terms of justice and peace. The project's originators did not intend to be indifferent to the essential task of making disciples, but their project was more to do with discipleship and conflict prevention which had its own integrity, relevance, statement of faith and appeal. From the outset, they felt the project was sufficiently strong in its own right and did not need to be given a label. Indeed specifying its Christian roots might have been divisive from the outset if it called on people with different allegiances to come together in the name of a faith which they did not share themselves.

Each day it became demonstrably clear on the sports fields that hundreds of people connected to communities of diverse faiths were glad to work together creatively with a common purpose and mutual accord; it was a 'bottom-up' demonstration and statement for others to consider.

What was of long-term importance was the relationship between Christians, Jews and Moslems as three religious bodies. During the project the subject of religion or religious affiliation was not raised or discussed. Yet the people from the three religions got on with a project and worked creatively together. If it had been necessary to have a discussion and agreement about the position of three faiths working closely together from a common position, it is to be questioned whether the project would have been possible, from the 'top-down' perspective. But because it was grounded from within the local community, and was 'bottom-up', it meant that people from the three faiths were engaged in a common project and found mutuality, trust and pleasure with each other. It can be argued that a stronger basis for encounters of a religious nature was provided when bridges of trust and confidence were created and found to work. The project demonstrated an informal, but real, ecumenicity and inter-religious dialogue on the ground. It created an atmosphere of confidence and trust to be carried into the future and stand as an example of hope within a country that held little optimism for the immediate or ultimate future.

Forgiveness and reconciliation

The project also expressed a vision of human sin, forgiveness and reconciliation in a relational context. It was hardly necessary to look for precise biblical definitions of sin; one vividly and starkly saw its awfulness in terms of relational solidarity as destructiveness passed on down the generations. In the context of the project at the time, it was awesome to witness the nature of hubris and superiority in relational and community terms, to say nothing of the racial overtones. Equally it pointed out some of the elements crucial to reconciliation – regret and apology (fresh words to replace penitence, and confession), forgiveness and genuine metanoia – a complete change of direction towards new ways of life and relationships. These are constructive replacements for resentment and punitive, authoritarian mindsets which otherwise contaminate relationships in the future. Such reconciliation often needs forgiveness, and probably costly forgiveness at that. It frequently involves the cost of not seeking revenge, of tolerating the pain of perceived atrocity, rather than returning it through vengeance and perpetuating the cycle of violence. People have to be sufficiently strong to have internalised the love of God, which reinforces them as they refrain from out-dated methods of reciprocal retaliation. This attitude of absorption is powerfully theological, being drawn directly from the non-retaliatory suffering of Christ as shown at Golgotha.[26]

Before forgiveness can become meaningful there needs to be some form of rapprochement. This might be brought about through the common experience of injury, but any sense that either side had committed acts worthy of forgiveness would take a combination of strength and humility. It was Isaiah the prophet who invited people with the words: '"Come now, let us reason together', says the Lord",[27] when he spoke of the sinner and the one sinned against. Reasonable listening and appreciation usually need to come about before forgiveness can be considered, and even before that the conditions for meetings to take place need to be created. With hindsight it was realised that the project actually enshrined 'breaking down the walls of partition'.[28] Such conditions would hardly have been likely if the communities had first needed to find political or credal agreement. Precisely at this juncture, the efficacy of the WSPP became profoundly relevant. A point of meeting with a mutually understood philosophy was provided for convivial experiences to be exchanged. People were brought together from diverse communities and faiths who wished to continue and expand the enterprise. This provided a stark contrast to what prevailed in other parts of the land, for it was peace making before the peace talking. The project created the conditions for people to speak and listen with those who would listen and speak. It provided an atmosphere of trust and confidence thus enabling genuine, creative encounter to take place. Because it was incarnational, reconciling and redemptive, it became a theology of hope in action.

Coincidences, providence and the Holy Spirit

It gradually emerged that the project was bigger than any one individual. Indeed one can look back and see what, in any other circumstance, would be deemed a 'coincidence', of things coming together at the same time, without any apparent links having been made. Time and again, coincidences occurred which made it possible to consider that there was a movement of God, an activity of the Holy Spirit, to which one could only respond with astonishment and gratitude. Thus there was a set of beliefs behind the project at its beginning and this chapter describes what emerged. Doubtless there will be more to follow.

The early understanding had to include extensions of the Genesis account of the Spirit brooding on the face of the Creation,[29] first moving without humanity and then going on to influence it. Thereafter, God continued to move creatively, before His people arrived at the same place and became freely enjoined in the design. There was an anticipation that the creative Spirit of God would continue to work and move in diverse ways beyond immediate awareness, and that ultimately the project belonged to Him. The essential nature of the awareness that He had brought the project from nowhere to substance, indicated not only His providence but His proactive involvement, before the prime movers of the project became aware of the evidence.

It was also true that the entrustment of the project to the British Council and the University of Brighton was 'an act of faith'.[30] If the project was the initiative of the Holy Spirit, the two co-founders were merely agents, although nonetheless, extremely proactive in the process. From the very outset, they had reckoned on passing the project, if it was successful, to a larger organisation which had the resources to take it even further forward. They had responded to its creation and would not see its completion, which was itself in the Christian tradition.[31] Thus while there were a number of concerns about the nature of the entrustment, as well as its future direction, the 'letting go' was also a theological attitude. It was an unspoken acknowledgement that the project was far bigger than any individuals, and it would follow a course which was not theirs to control, but could be left to God as it was entrusted to others.

Political theology, incarnation, servanthood and society

One subject which would have found little common connection between the three Abrahamic faiths had it been discussed, was that of the suffering of God; to have introduced it would very likely have halted any creative activity. While it was not a subject that was ready to be raised, the issue of suffering was ever present in the background of the project. The suffering of the Jews in the Holocaust is well documented, and the suffering of the Palestinians less so, although that has increasingly changed.[32] Moltmann quotes Elie Wiesel,[33] a survivor of Auschwitz, as he spoke of the death of three Jews hanged by the SS. One was a boy who took longer to die and lasted half an hour. Moltmann develops the theme of the God who suffers. "To speak here of a God who could not suffer would make God a demon".[34] Just as he spoke of the God who suffered with imprisoned Jews, surely God similarly suffered with Arabs when Jews were reported as imprisoning, persecuting and murdering them in Israel.

The project could well be seen as an expression of Political Theology. It went into the arena of suffering and stood side by side with the fearful, the oppressed and the oppressor and, without condemnation, offered creative alternatives of reconciling influence. Moltmann is clear in his understanding that the suffering God in Christ identifies with suffering humanity. He states:

> *The memory of the passion and resurrection of Christ is at the same time both dangerous and liberating. It endangers a church which is adapted to the religious politics of its time and brings it into fellowship with the sufferers of its time.*[35]

The WSPP encapsulated and acted out that profound truth without specifically mentioning it by word; it demonstrated it in action for over three years.

In summary, the project was more than humanism. It did not need to be advertised as Christian – that was another matter. It had its own flow and did not need to be displayed. It was self-evident and that was sufficient. If people saw their good works and glorified their father in heaven,[36] so be it. The WSPP was incarnational because it did not extract people from their trauma or desperation. Instead it went to people, and lived with them in their predicament, while enabling them to experience another way of community life.[37] This project may have had its shortcomings, insofar as each annual project lasted only about ten days, but it created a model which could be continued without the presence of the team from the UK. It was intended that the communities would be empowered, and that they would continue to interact after the UK team's departure, thus developing the concept with others. It provided a working model of confidence and hope for the future.

The project was also charismatic; it was possible to trust that not only would a person be guided, but also sustained, by God's Spirit – thus they could endure and persevere at the task. Moreover, there was what might be called a domino effect, in that the Spirit acted with a network of people, and others were equally led, and moved to do apparently unconnected things as part of a whole. Communities of people came together and went away to meet again and again. They were moved to create projects in

160

subsequent years that others in the region could not even contemplate. At the start of the Occupation, or the outbreak of the Intifada, it would have been unthinkable. But from within their midst a new dimension for creative life together had arisen.

The concept of servanthood meant no more striving for control in leadership. It was a privilege beyond price to be part of a project that did not involve payment, simply the flow of one's creativity, care and commitment. This spilled over into the way one conducted relationships and interpersonal dealings in upholding values that were constructive, kind, loving, ethical, moral and honest. It did not need to be successful; only faithful, as befitted the 'stewards of the mysteries of God'.[38]

Thus proselytism, or conversion, was not relevant – the project was created out of an identifiable need. "Hope was reckoned to be when one did what was needed, not because it was to be successful but because it was the right thing to do."[39] There was a destiny with which to become enjoined, in terms of both the Lord's Prayer,[40] and St Paul's letter to the Church at Ephesus,[41] and in terms of the fulfilment of God's ultimate purpose for the cosmos.

The outcome meant that people came together for a team sport which all had enjoyed beforehand. No demands were made on participants in credal terms; people were invited to join, with everyone observing the rules of football. Thus they all had something in common, whatever their background. The project was inclusive of everyone within a certain age range and beyond that, there was no exclusiveness. They put aside their individualism in order to work with each other in the community life of a team. They created a fresh spirit themselves, among themselves. They returned triumphant to their homes and communities, and reappeared the next day to be with people, trusted colleagues and fellow team members, while elsewhere, people from the same backgrounds were estranged. A new dimension of societal attitudes was created. In finding a fresh way of conducting relationships, it modelled the way for future societal relationships and problem solving. This was distinctively different from what was going on in other places, where, despite great earnestness, people who came from suspicious and hostile communities had to sit at the same table as strangers to begin talks about peace. In the Galilee, at the World Sports Peace Project, people sat down with comrades and friends. There was a different atmosphere, not because of credal statements but because of the common ground and mutual bonds they had created together through amiable and collective contact over a significant period of time.

This chapter has identified some of the theological influences that initiated, drove and sustained the project until its successful completion. Just as St Paul once described the division between God and humanity, and Jews and Gentiles being broken down by Christ, so it was possible to see something more of this reflected in the project, in terms of 'destroying the barriers, the dividing wall of hostility'.[42]

It has already been stated that the WSPP had no need of labels for the purposes of identification. In essence it reconciled and carried hope for all who were to become involved in future years. The relevance of Christianity, indeed all ethical religions, was invisibly demonstrated and the project was acknowledged, both publicly and internationally, to be successful. Imperceptibly, it was one more small step for humankind.

List of the WSPP Coaching Teams, 2001–2003

JULY 2001
University of Brighton: Senior Coach, Gary Stidder.
Eamon Brennan, Emma Day, Helen Goodacre, Russell LeFoevre, Charlotte Mills, Craig Northedge.
Also, Michelle Donnelly, Olympic Aid; Steven Fine, Maimonides Foundation; Patrick Johnson, Researcher, University of Brighton.
WSPP: Geoffrey Whitfield.

AUGUST 2002
University of Brighton: Senior Coaches: John Sugden, Gary Stidder.
Eamon Brennan, Helen Goodacre, Simon Hinchcliffe, Chris Howarth, Sharon McSwegan, Naomi Poletyllo, James Scott, Steve Smith.
WSPP: Geoffrey Whitfield.

JULY 2003
University of Brighton: Senior Coaches: John Sugden, Gary Stidder, John Lambert.
Dave Carney, James Clarke, Adrian Haasner, Simon Hinchcliffe, Chris Howarth, Dan Rose.
University of Brunel: Gary Armstrong, Lecturer; Alexandre Serpente, Iyla Macintyre, Trevor Humphreys, Luke Nicholls.
St Mary's College, Twickenham, The University of Surrey: Bernadette Woods, Tracey Kevins.
Southampton Institute of Higher Education: Kim Wilmshurst.
Film Crew: Director, Carl Dearing; Ben Davidson, Anthony Batchelor.
WSPP: Geoffrey Whitfield.

Notes

1 His Excellency Sherard Cowper-Coles, Her Majesty's Ambassador to Israel, in his speech given at the prize-giving after the third Tournament, Kfar Tavor, Israel, 11 July 2003.
2 Psalm 37, v. 23.
3 This was a prelude to the creation of The World Sports Peace Project a few months later, after Geoffrey and David met Johann Olav Koss of Olympic Aid at Heathrow on 4 March 2001.
4 St John, Ch. 15, vv. 1–17.
5 Ephesians, Ch. 1, v. 10.
6 It means here that one relates the past to the present and vice versa, and so the past and present tenses change as they interact.
7 A. Richardson & J. Bowden (eds.), *The Westminster Dictionary of Christian Theology* (Philadelphia: The Westminster Press, 1983), p. 498. Also quoted by O. McTernan *Violence in God's Name* (London: Darton, Longman and Todd, 2003), p. xvi.
8 St John, Ch. 15, vv. 1–9.
9 O. McTernan, *Violence in God's Name* (London: Darton, Longman & Todd, 2003), p. 159.
10 II Corinthians, Ch. 1, v. 4.
11 King Jnr., Martin Luther, *The Autobiography of Martin Luther King Jnr.* (London: Abacus, 2000).
12 Exodus, Ch. 14, v. 13.
13 St John, Ch. 6, v. 9.
14 Jeremiah, Ch. 31, v. 33.
15 St Matthew, Ch. 6, v. 10.
16 "Ultimate accountability". A term, possibly not new, but coined during discussion between Geoffrey Whitfield and Oliver McTernan when they first met in London, 13 September 2004.
17 Genesis, Ch. 8.
18 St Matthew, Ch. 6, v. 10.
19 Genesis, Ch. 1, v. 22, Ch. 8, v. 17.

20 This tension was seen to emerge in Chapter 5, entitled: 'An Act of Faith – the Entrustment'.

21 W. Bion, *Experiences in Groups* (London: Tavistock, 1961).

22 St Matthew, Ch. 5, v. 37.

23 The story of Achan and his family in Joshua Chapter 7. It is possible to interpret that whole action and its reflection of solidarity as based not on strength, but on fear of consequences and their wider implications.

24 Druze are very secretive about their beliefs and only a few selected leaders know their principles. Their roots are in Islam but they relate to those to whom they feel the closest at any one time, whether Moslem, Christian or Jew. See W. Dalrymple, *From the Holy Mountain* (London: Flamingo, 1998).

25 St Matthew, Ch. 6, v. 10.

26 I Peter, Ch. 2, vv. 23, 24.

27 Isaiah, Ch. 1, v. 18.

28 Ephesians, Ch. 2, v. 14.

29 Genesis, Ch. 1, v. 2.

30 These were the exact words of David Bedford to Geoffrey Whitfield as they discussed the "Entrustment" in September 2003.

31 St John, Ch. 3, v. 8.

32 U. Davis, *Apartheid Israel* (London: Zed, 2003).

33 E. Wiesel, *Night* (Harmondsworth Penguin: 1969), p. 75ff.

34 J. Moltmann, *The Crucified God* (London: SCM, 1974), pp. 273, 274.

35 J. Moltmann, *The Crucified God* (London: SCM, 1974), p. 326. See also G. A. Studdert-Kennedy, *High and Lifted Up* from *The Unutterable Beauty* (London: Hodder & Stoughton, 1931).

36 St Matthew, Ch. 5, v. 16.

37 There are fine organisations that take people from their communities and give them the space to look from a distance at the situation from which they have come For example, the Corymeela Community in Northern Ireland and the Seeds of Peace organisation in New York City.

38 I Corinthians, Ch. 4, vv. 1, 2.

39 Taken from President Havel of Czechoslovakia by Rt. Rev. R. Harries, the Bishop of Oxford, September 2004, in the BBC Radio Four Today programme.

40 St Matthew, Ch. 6, v. 10, *"Your will be done on earth."*

41 Ephesians, Ch. 1, v. 10, *"when the times will have reached their fulfilment – to bring all things in heaven and on earth together."*

42 Ephesians, Ch. 2, v. 14.

Sources and References

Bion, W., *Experiences in Groups* (London: Tavistock, 1961).

Bowen, J., *Six Days* (London: Simon & Schuster, 2003).

Chacour, E., with Hazard D., *Blood Brothers* (New York: Chosen, 1984).

Dalrymple, W., *From the Holy Mountain* (London: Flamingo, 1997).

Foiuda, Y. & Fielding, N., *Masterminds of Terror* (Edinburgh: Mainstream, 2003).

King, Jnr., M. L., *The Autobiography of Martin Luther King Jnr.* (London: Abacus, 2000).

King, Jnr., M. L., *The Strength to Love* (New York: Harper & Row, 1963).

La Guardia, A., *Holy Land, Unholy War* (London: John Murray, 2002).

McTernan, O., *Violence in God's Name* (London: Darton Longman & Todd, 2003).

Reeve, S., *One Day in September* (London: Faber, 2000).

Richardson, A. & Bowden, J. (eds) *The Westminster Dictionary of Christian Theology* (Philadelphia: The Westminster Press, 1983).

Studdert-Kennedy, G. A., *The Unutterable Beauty* (London: Hodder & Stoughton, 1927).

Sugden, J. & Bairner, A., eds., *Sport in Divided Societies* (Oxford: Meyer & Meyer, 2000).

Index

169

Dave Bedford during his 10,000m World Record Run in 1973. This project has been supported by David throughout, whose knowledge and experience in sport has helped in the creation of a unique, grassroots project, which was not only successful in the Middle East but could be transferred to anywhere in the world and bring a different quality of life and hope for all those caught up in violence and conflict.